For my son, *Oliver*

emotions *in between* emotions

Steve *Dean* Mendes

Hope

A tear
Tore apart
The mask,
Too tight to breathe
To loose to hide.
Fragile crystal orbits
Reflect, Deflect, Shatter.

In a dream,
A thought,
A wish,
Pain dissipates
Despair petrifies
Lazarus ale
Bathes our soul.

A path,

Lightened by torches,

Extinct ashes from burned sorrow.

Smoke roams.

Transforms,

Destroys,

Existence surpasses the I.

An inner beating,

Awakens.

A warm heart,

Peels.

Cracked layers,

Fall.

Gratitude,

Hope,

Love,

Uncovers the Self.

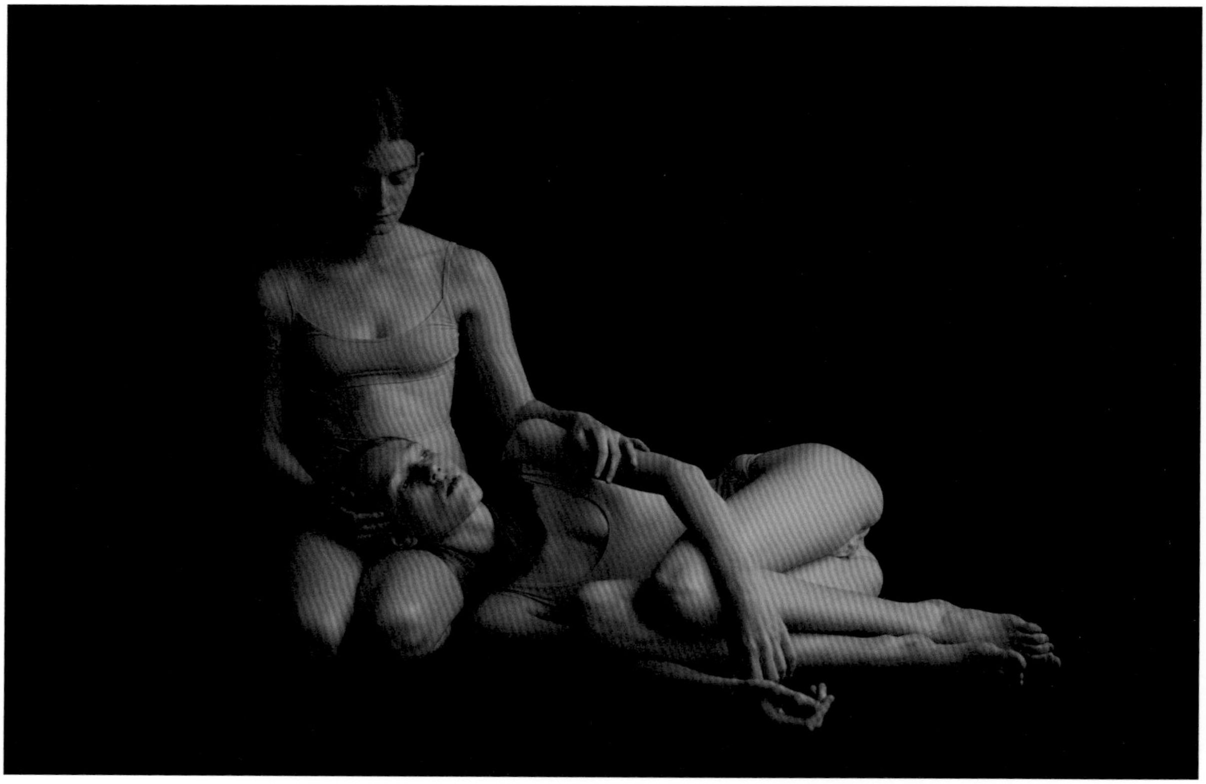

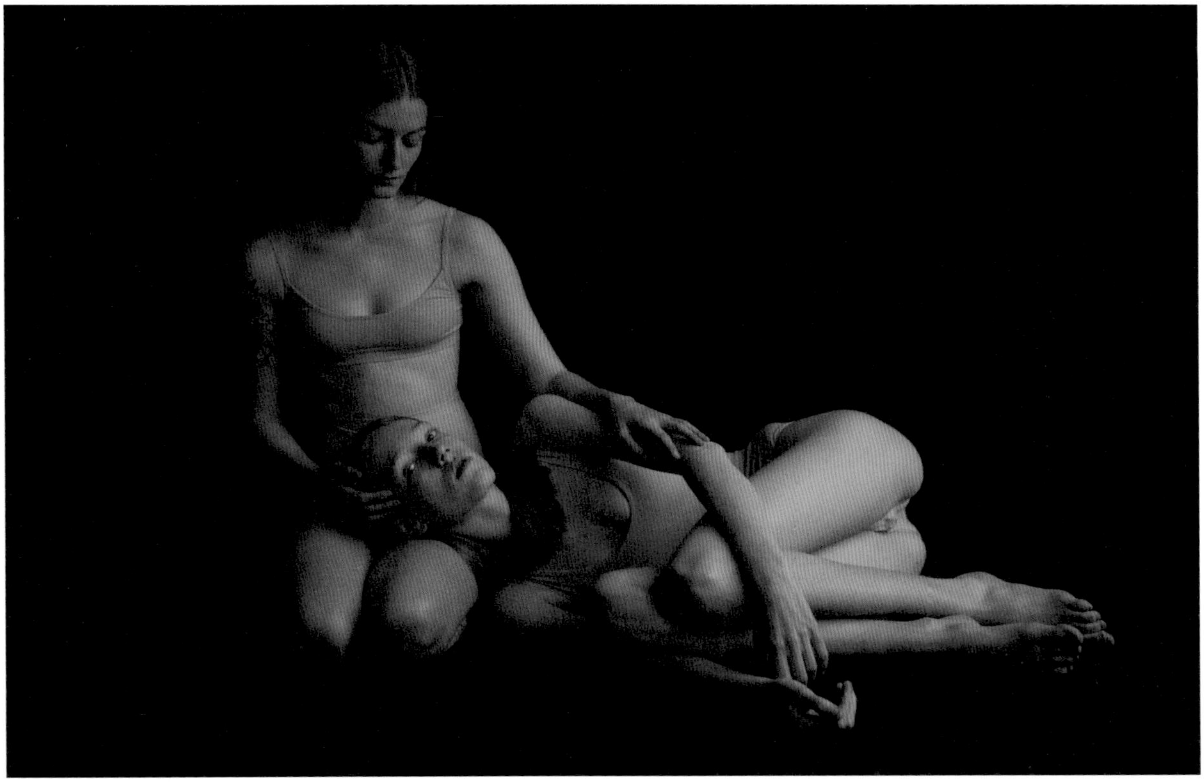

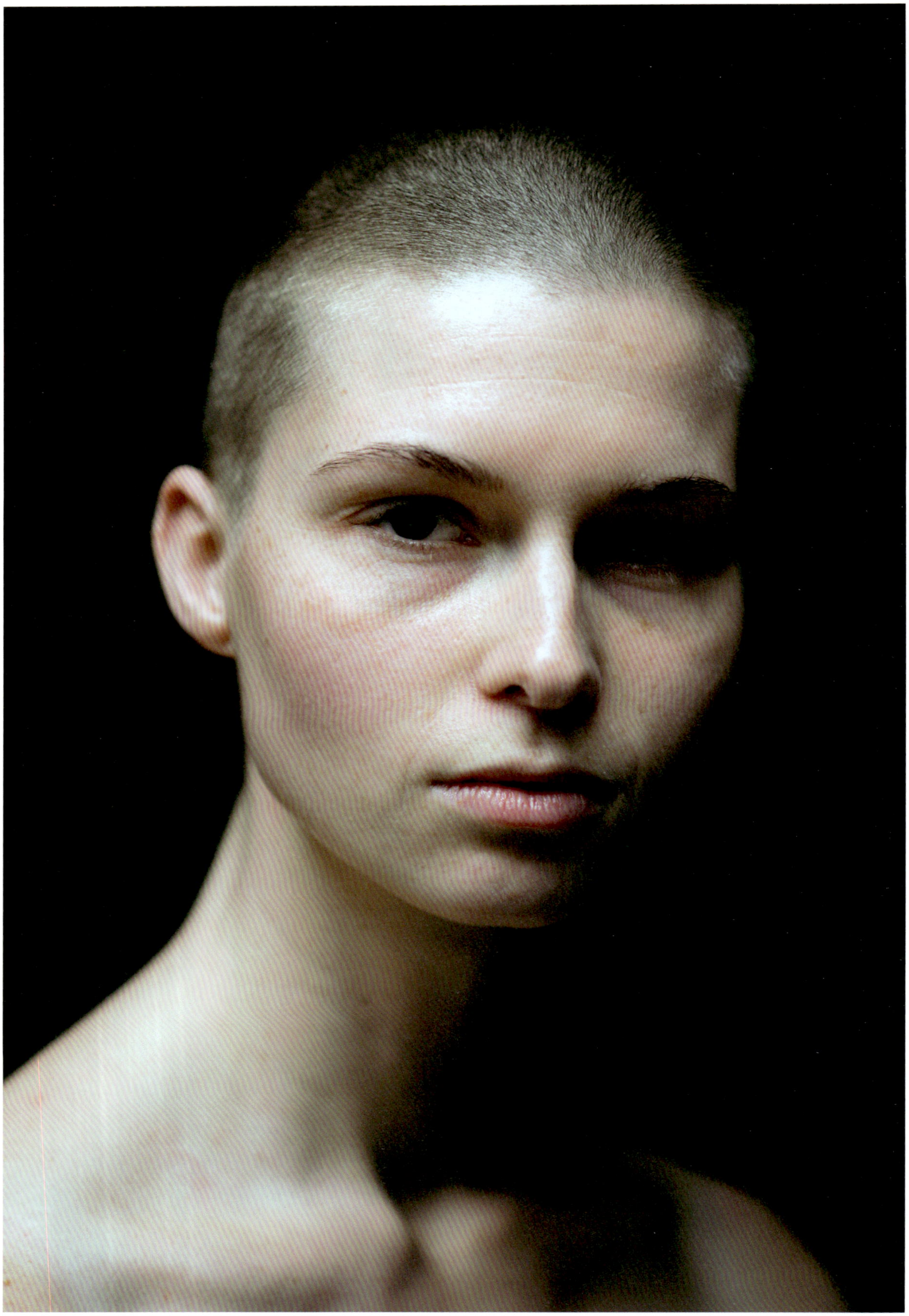

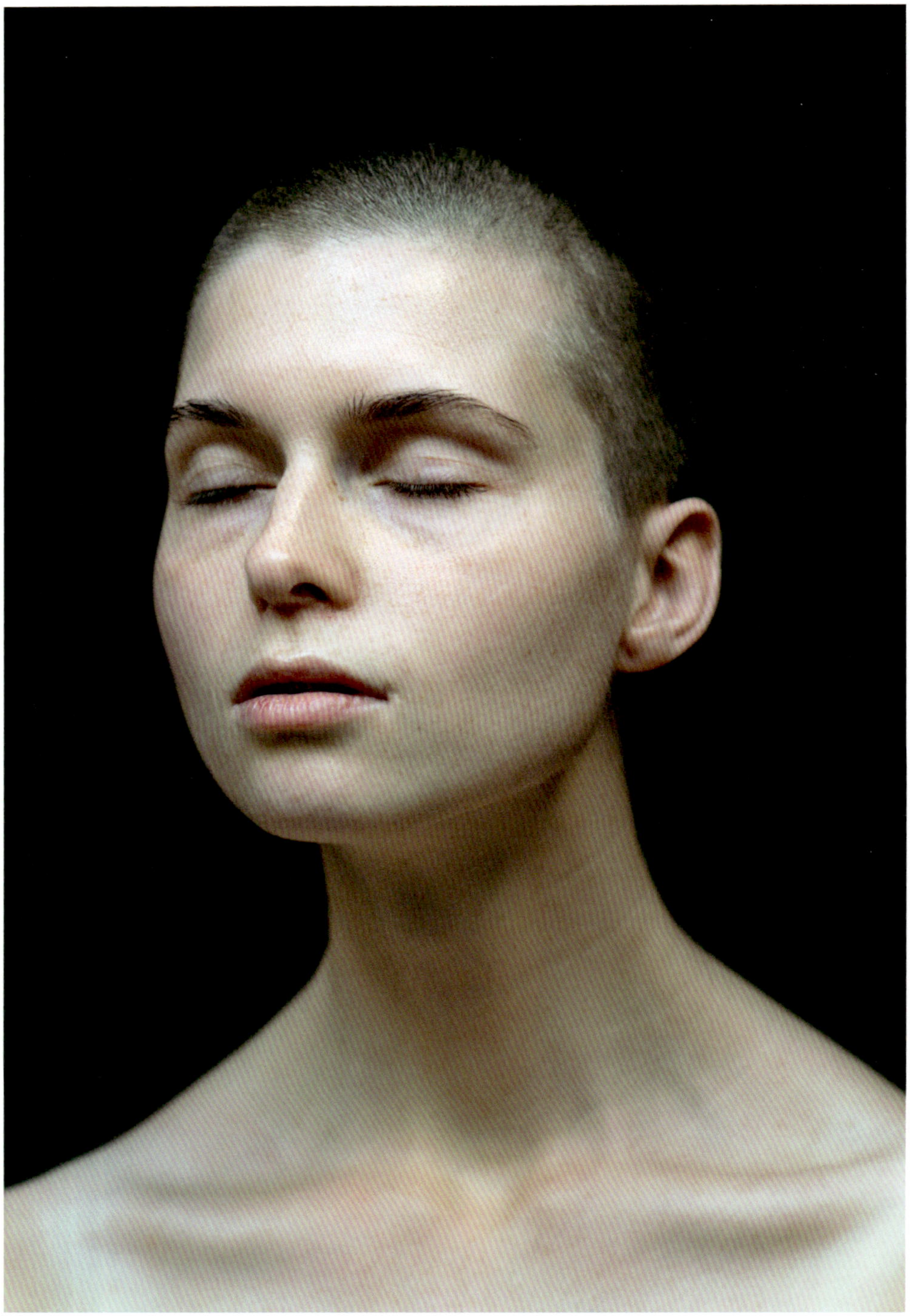

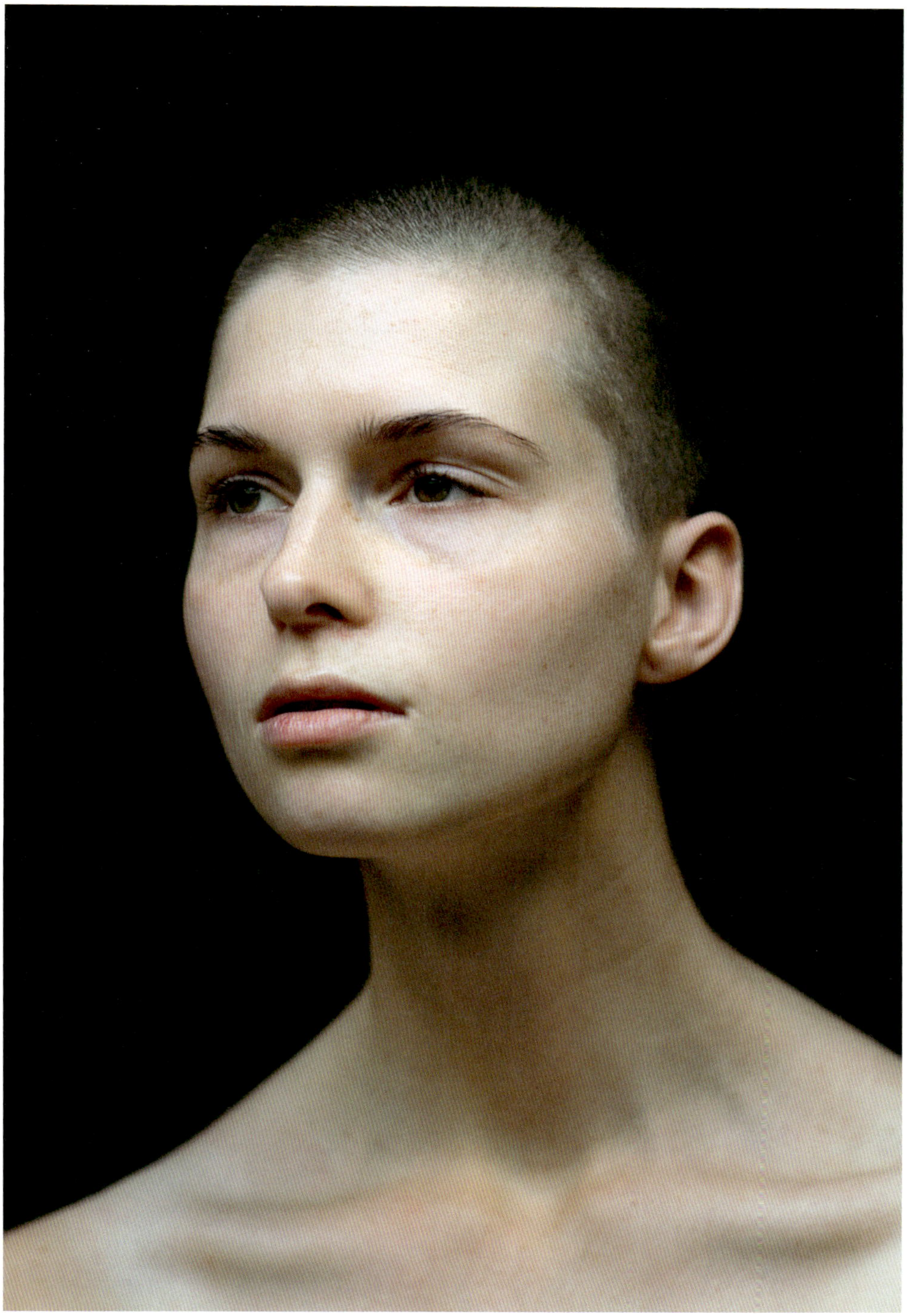

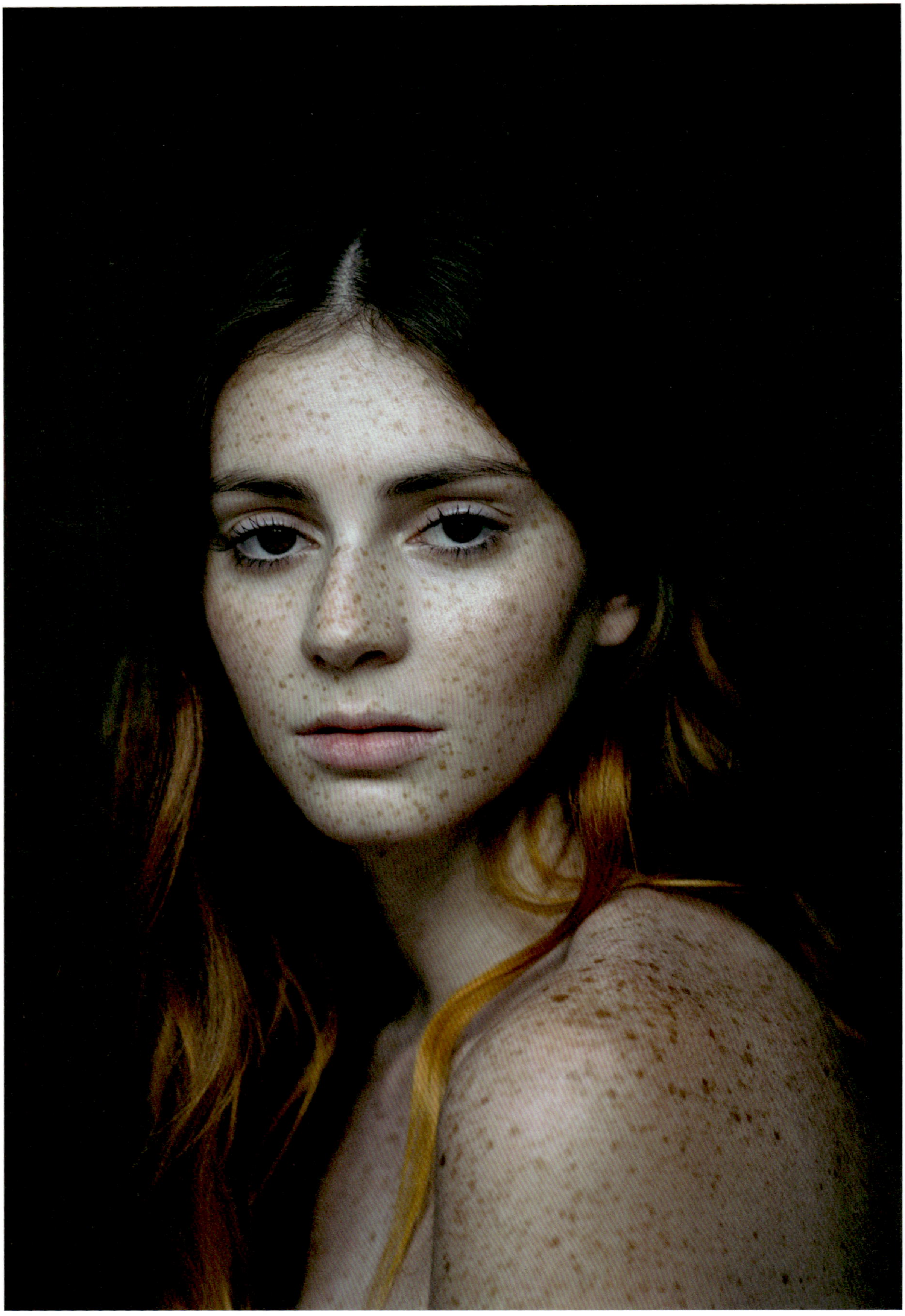

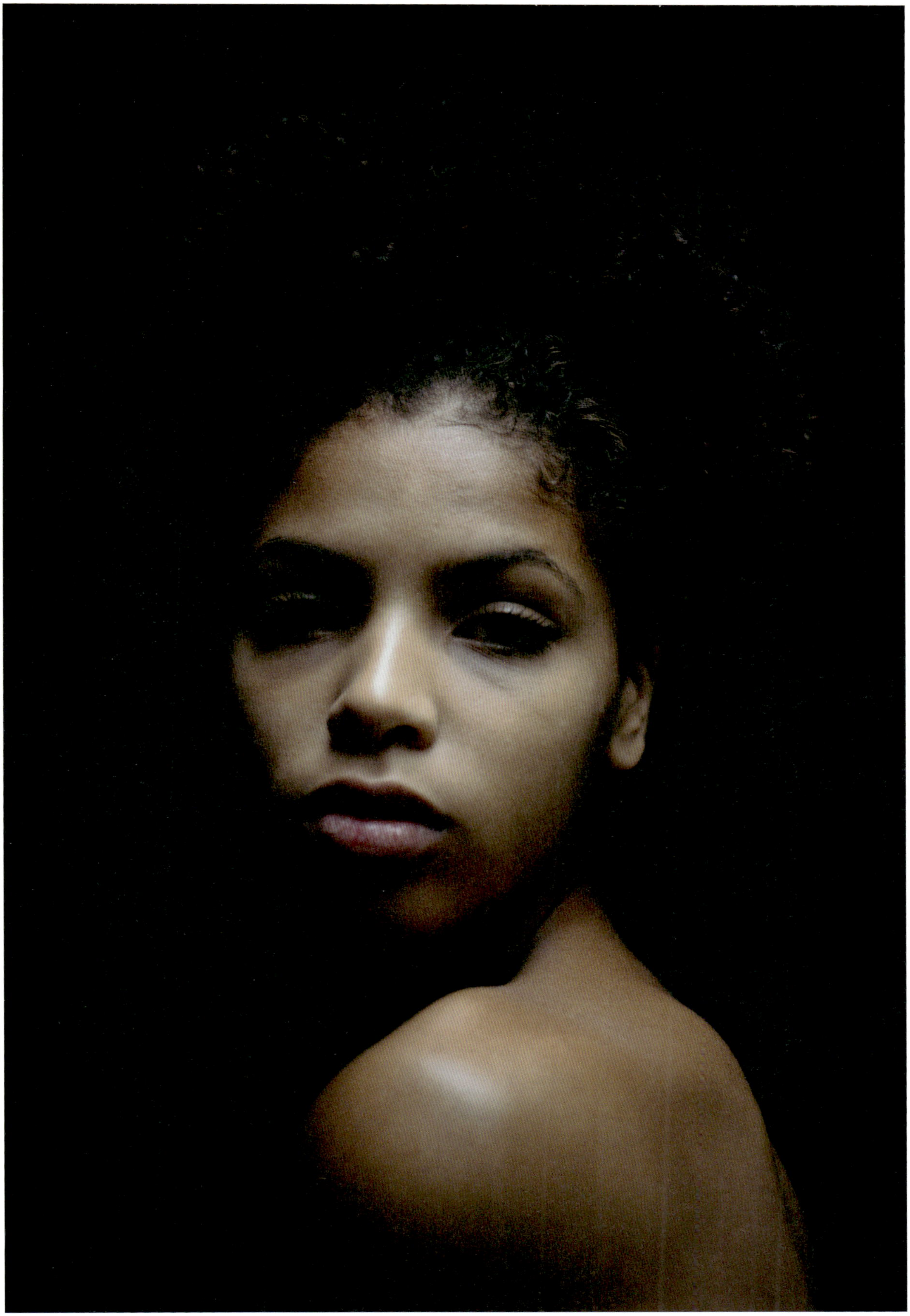

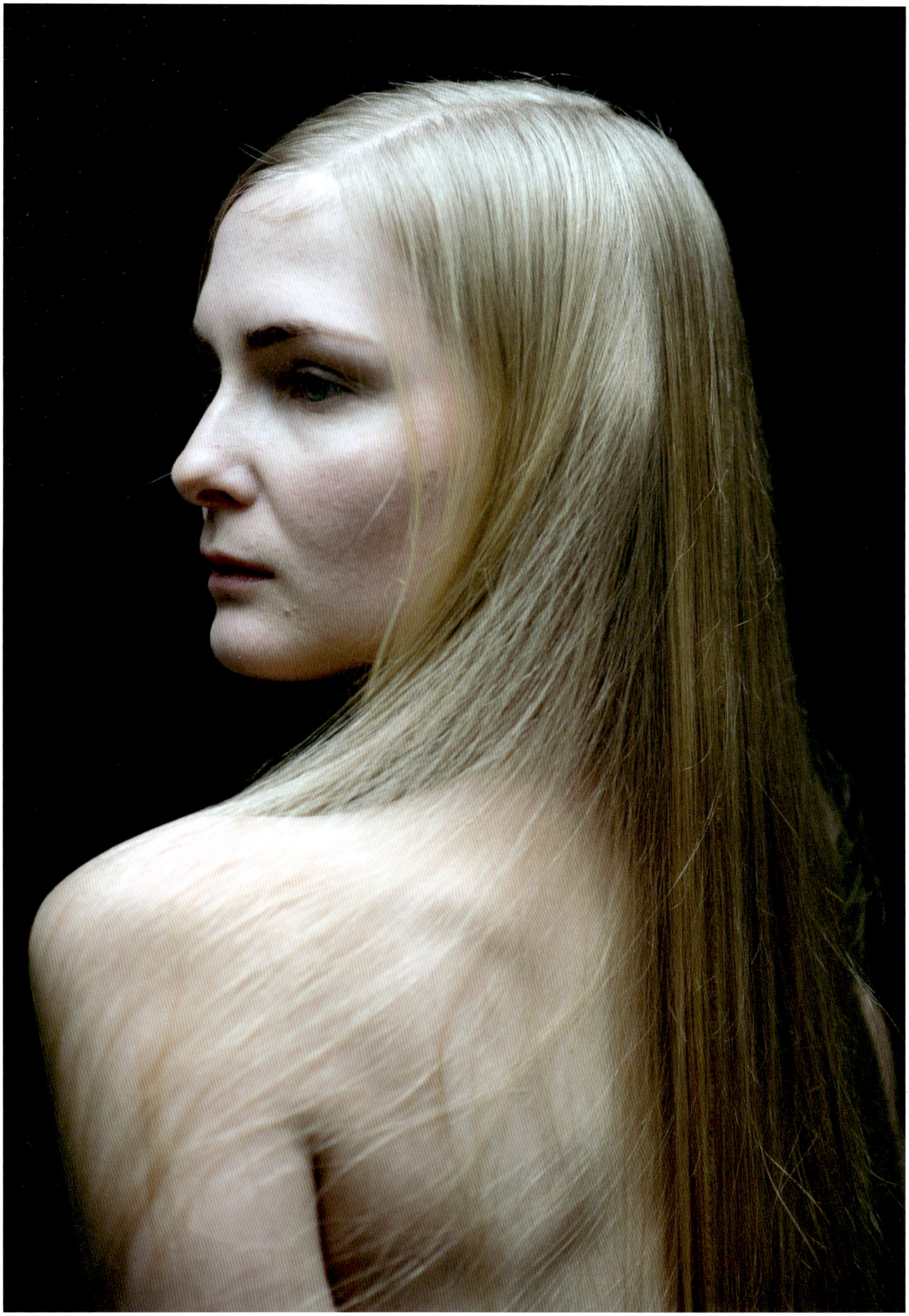

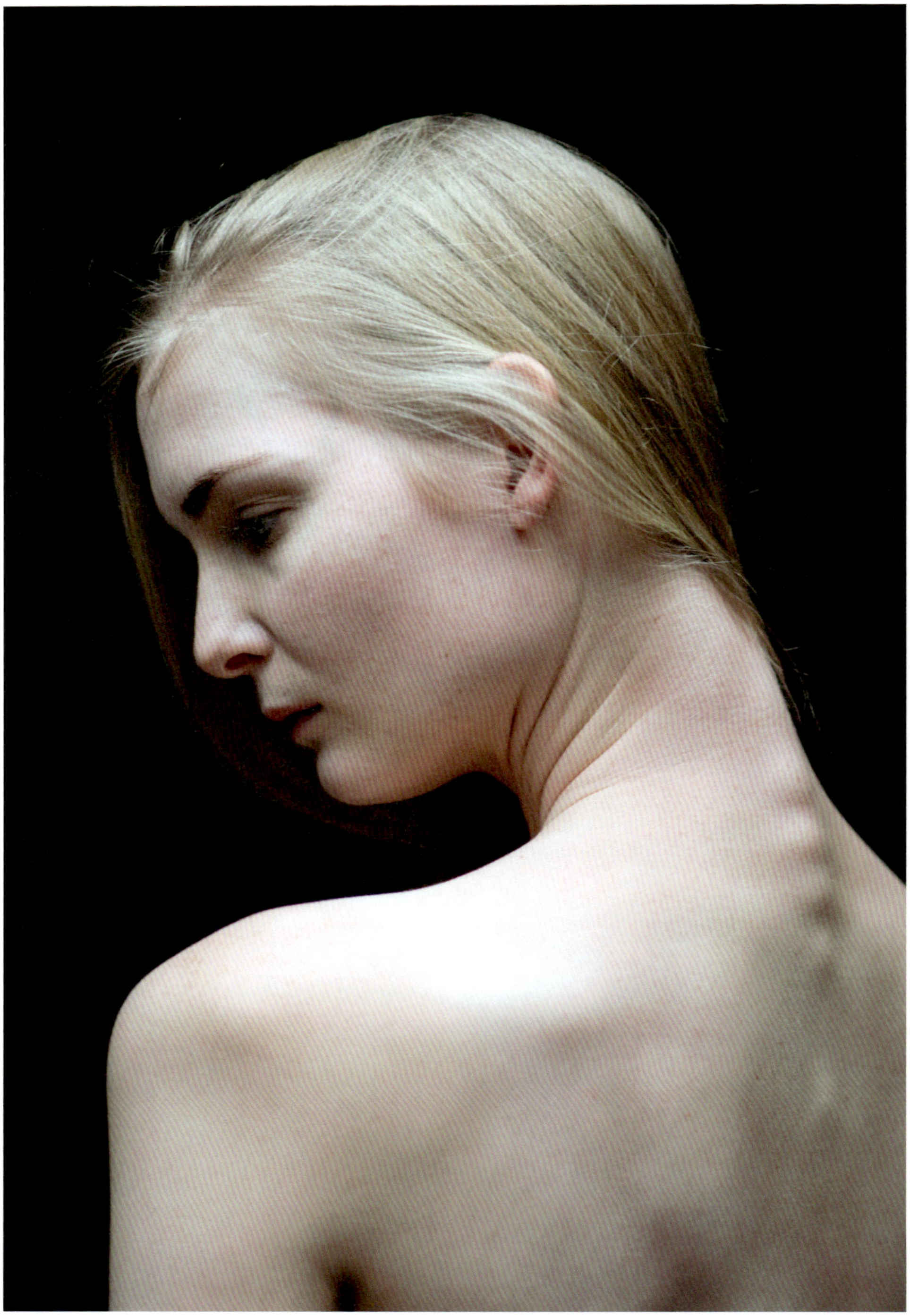

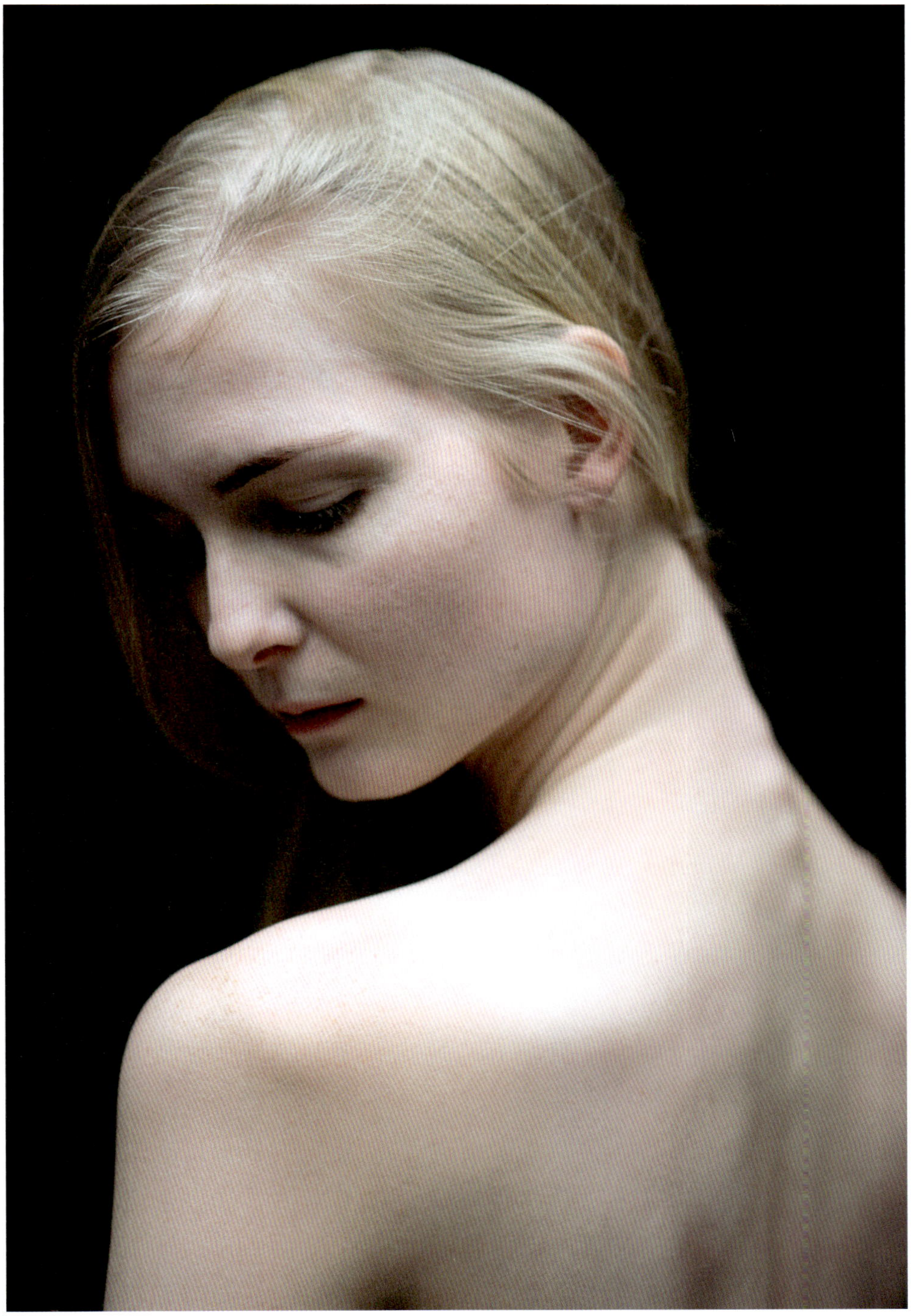

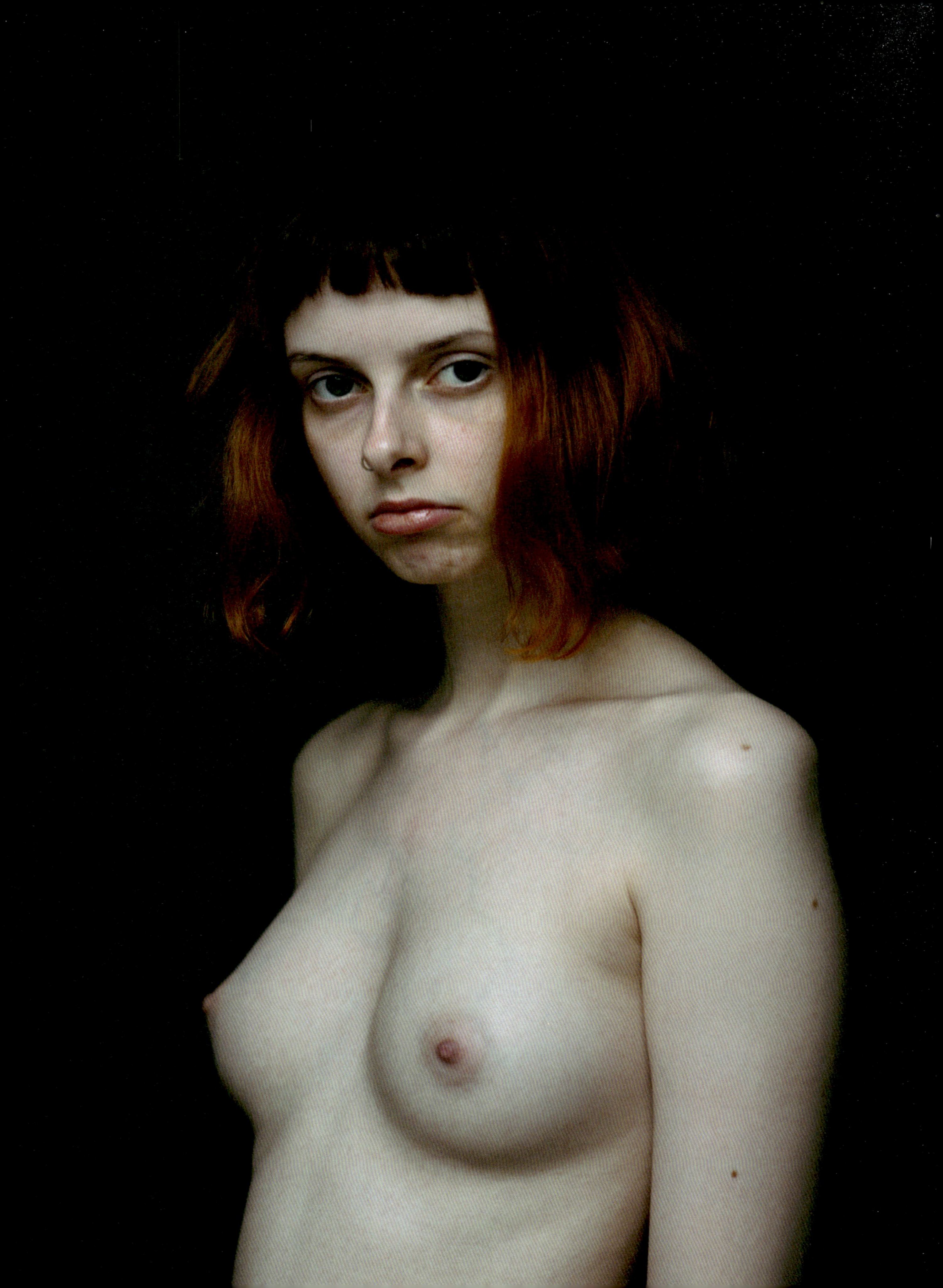

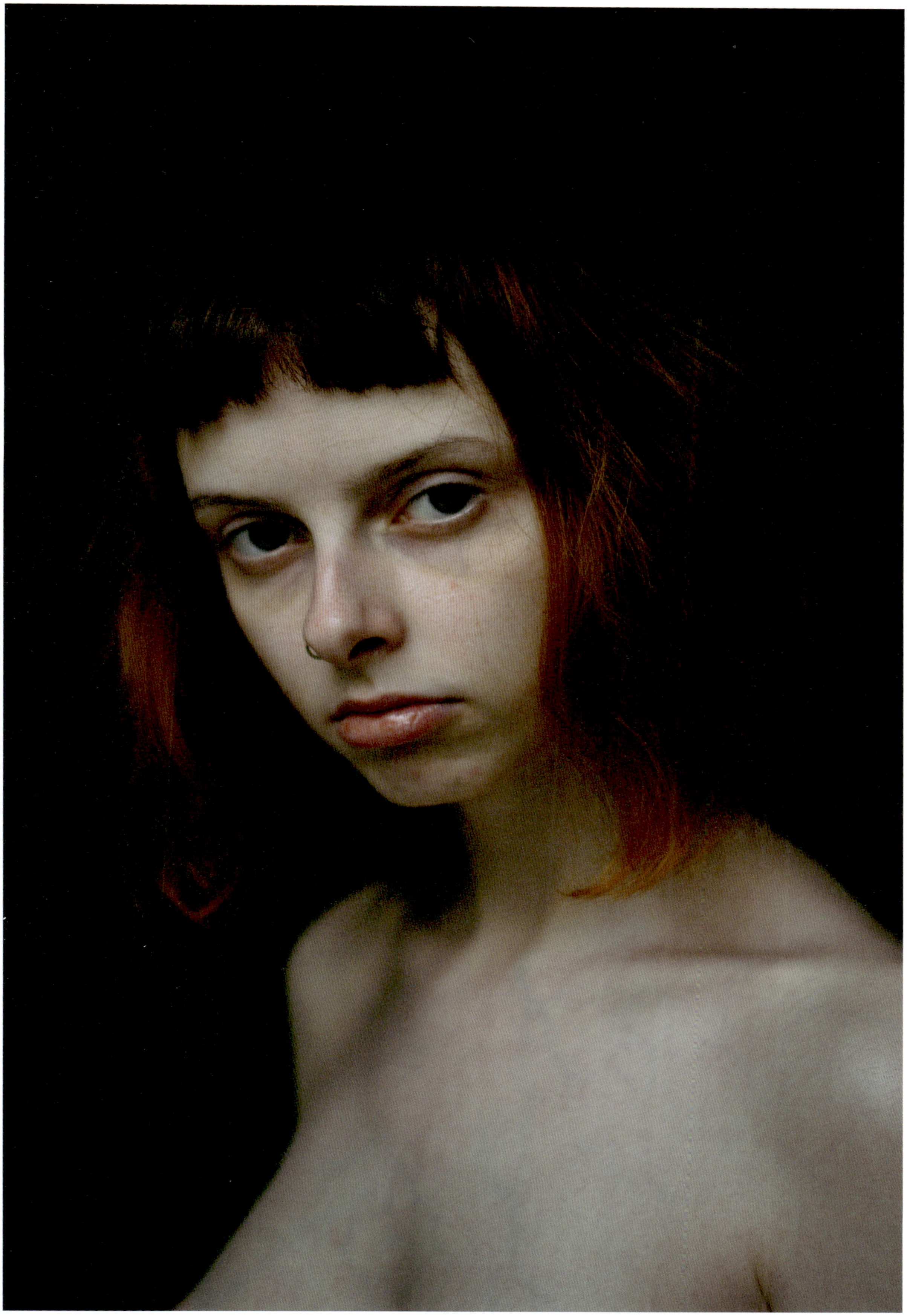

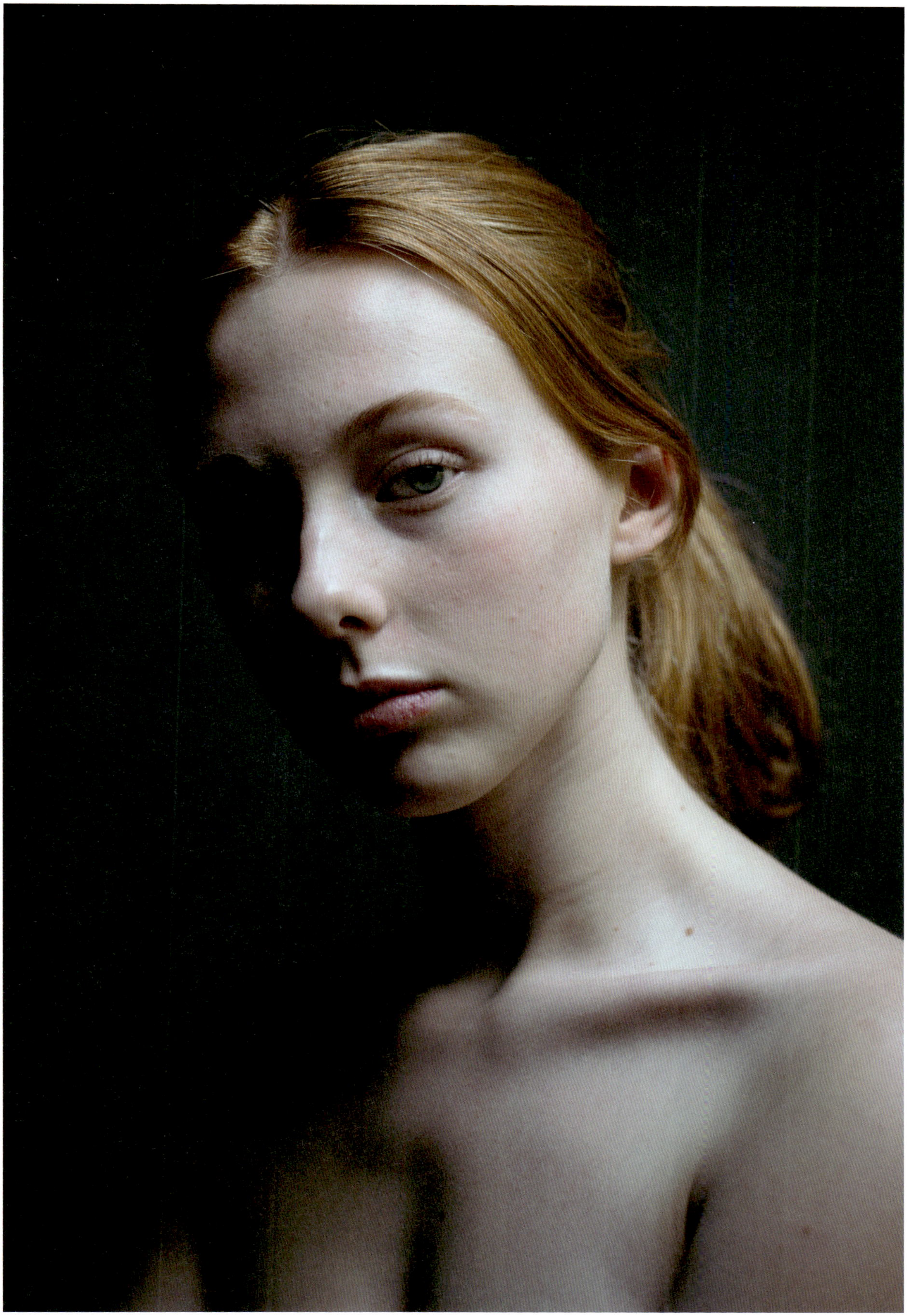

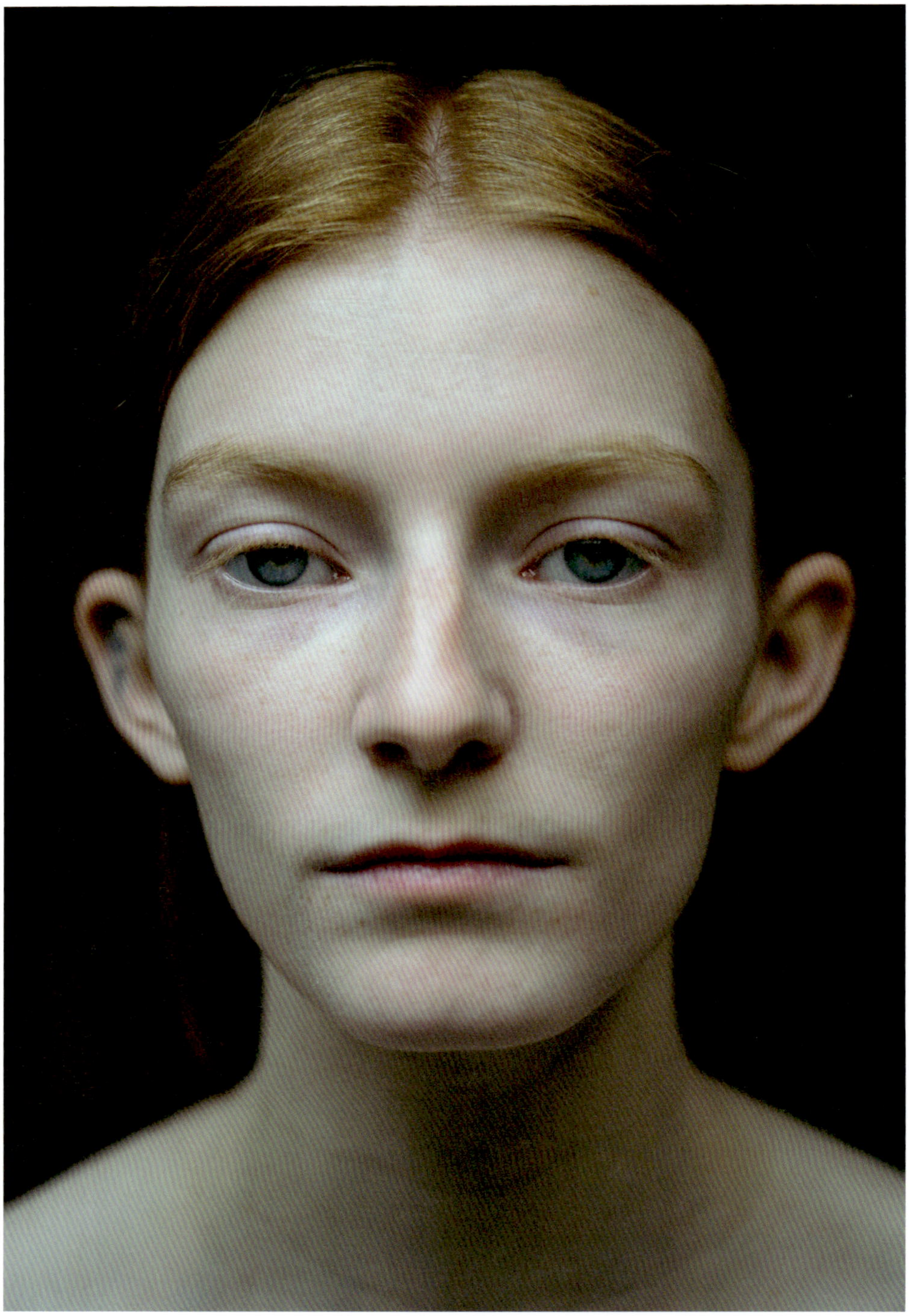

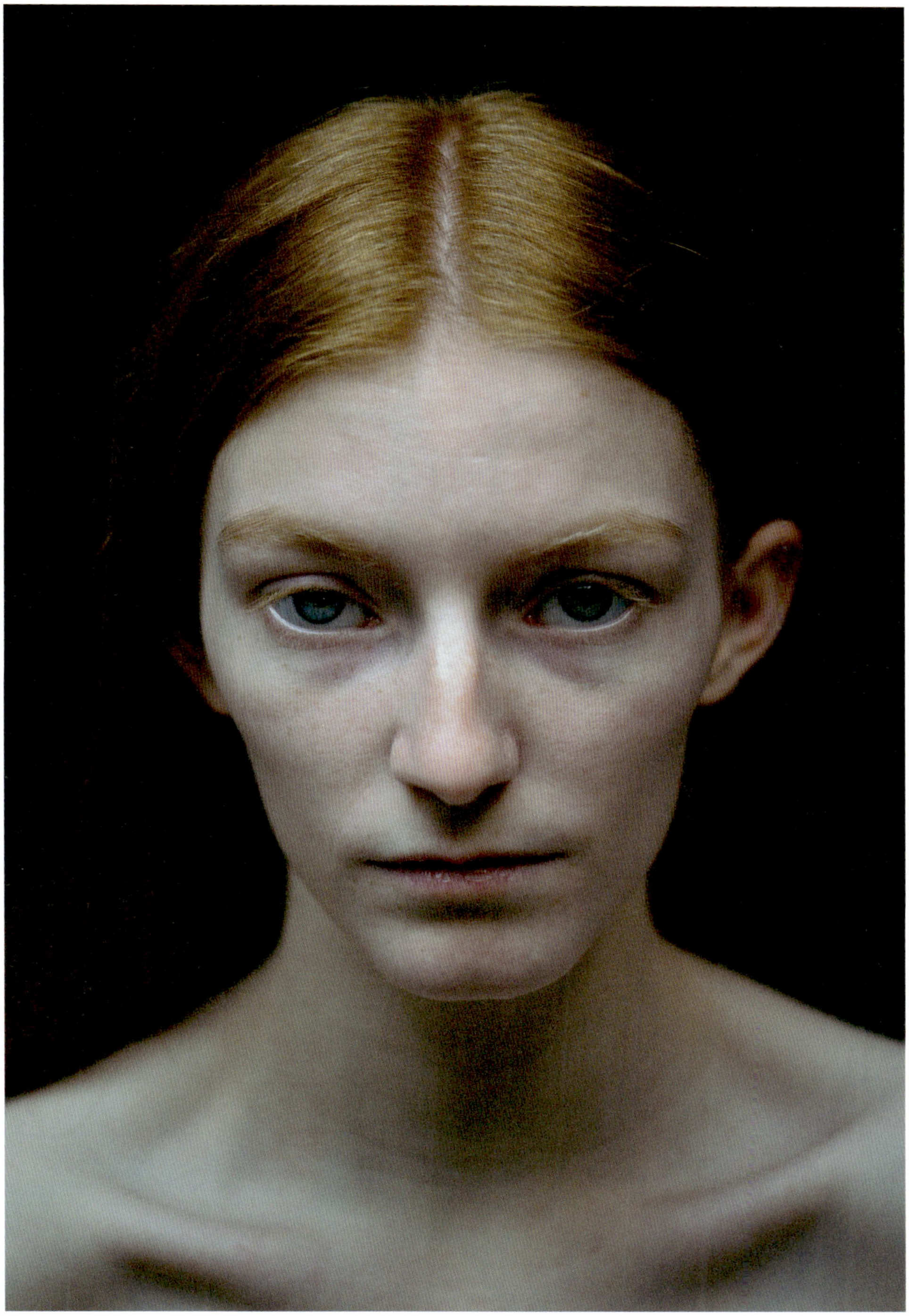

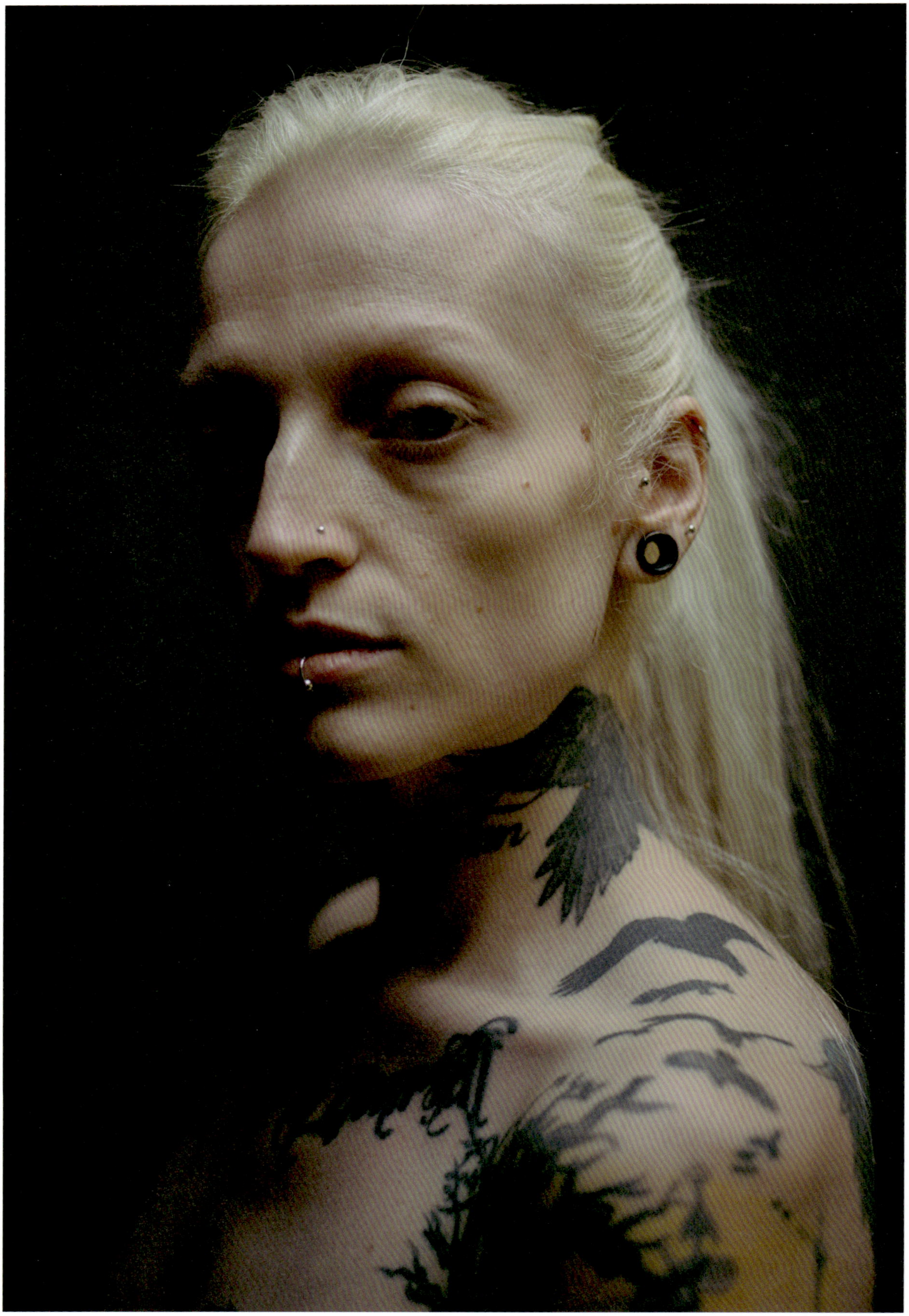

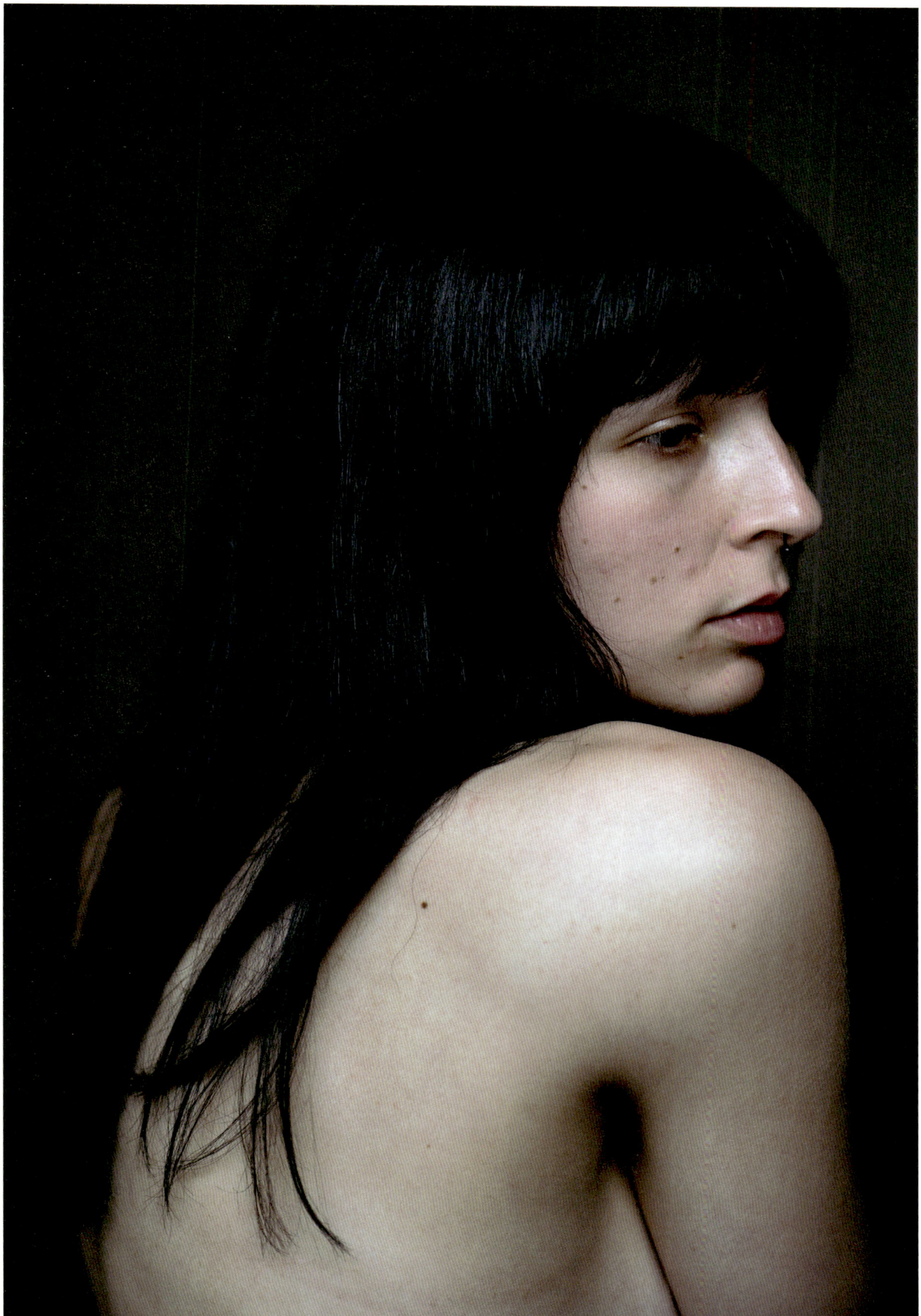

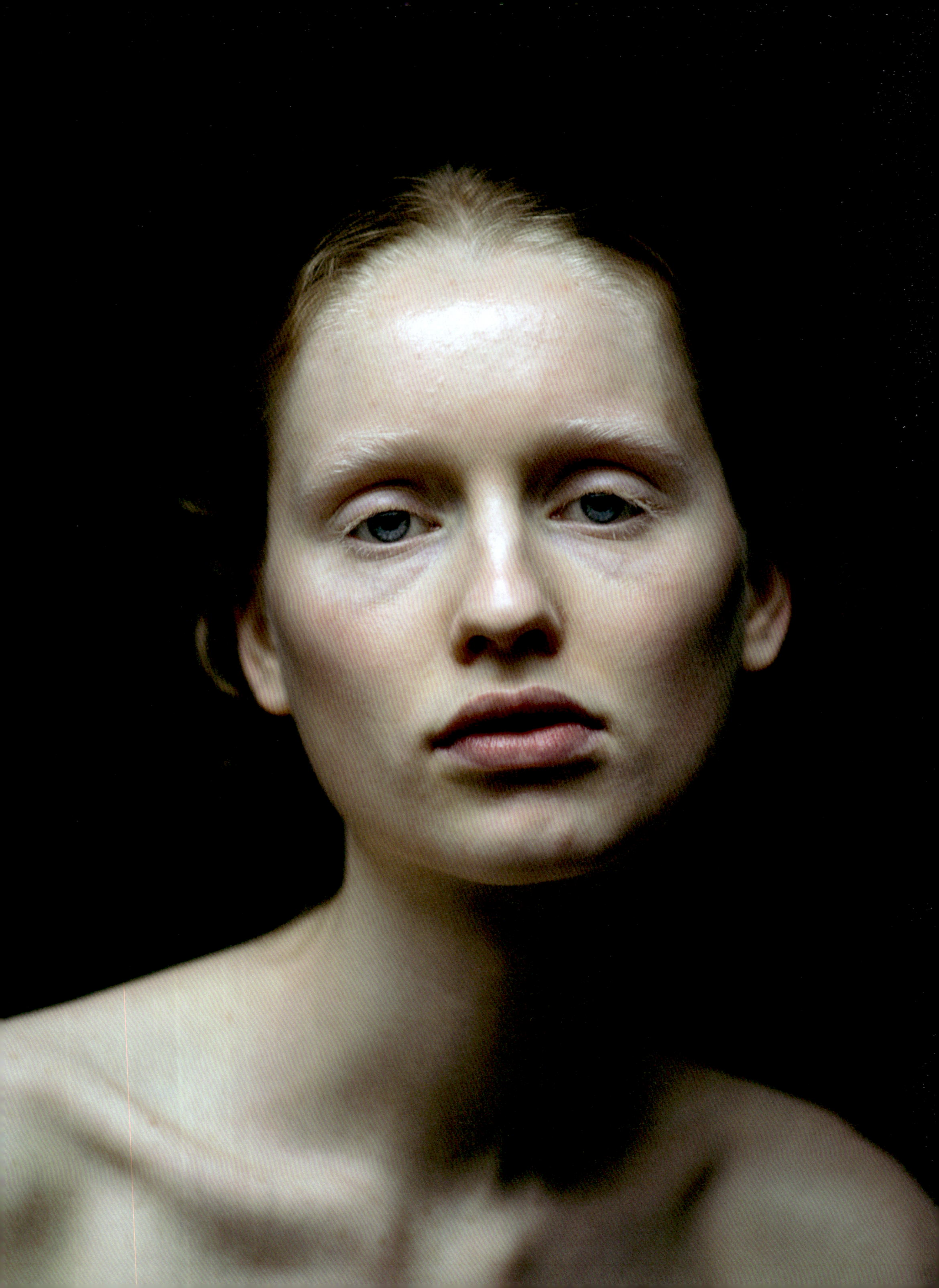

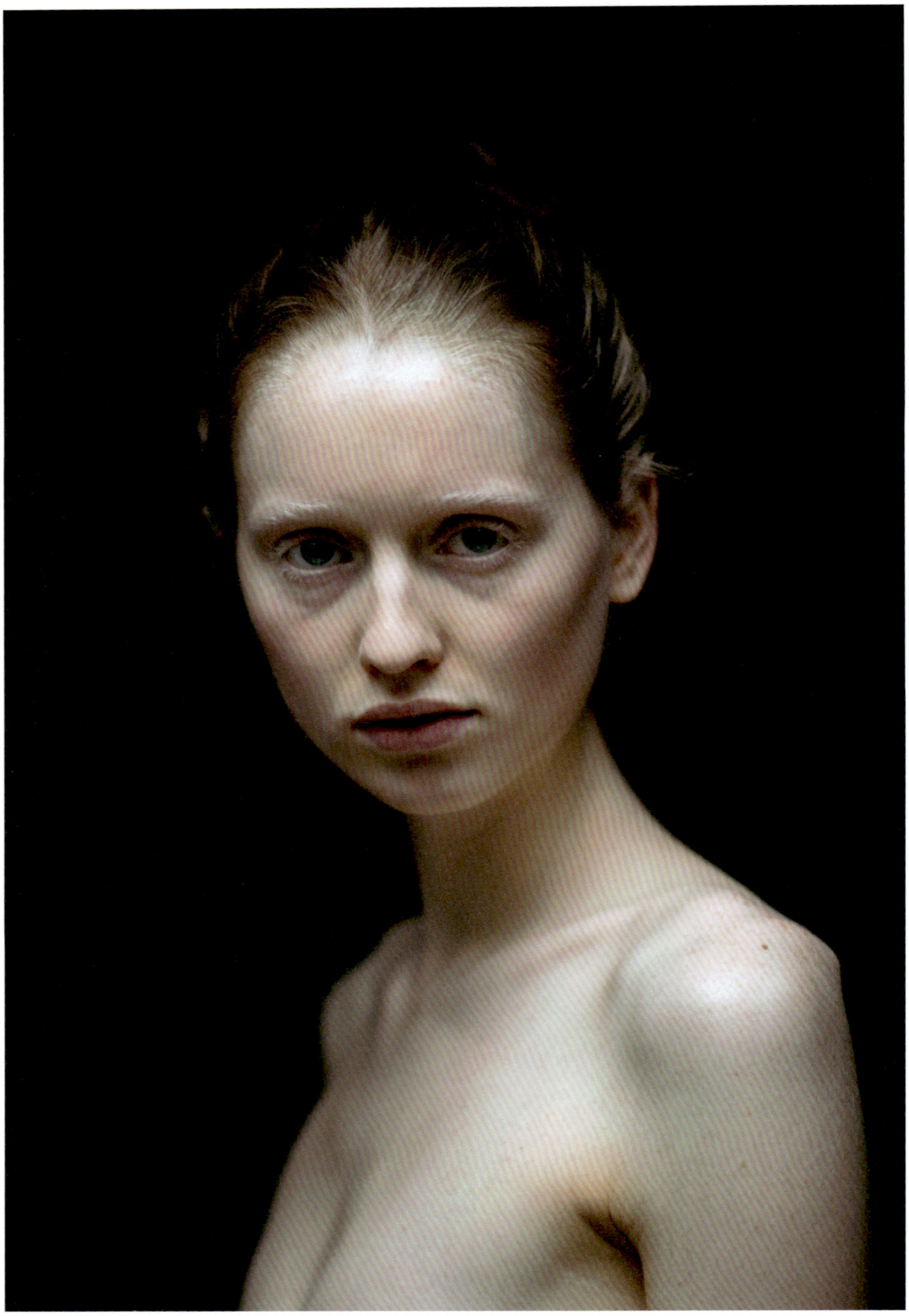

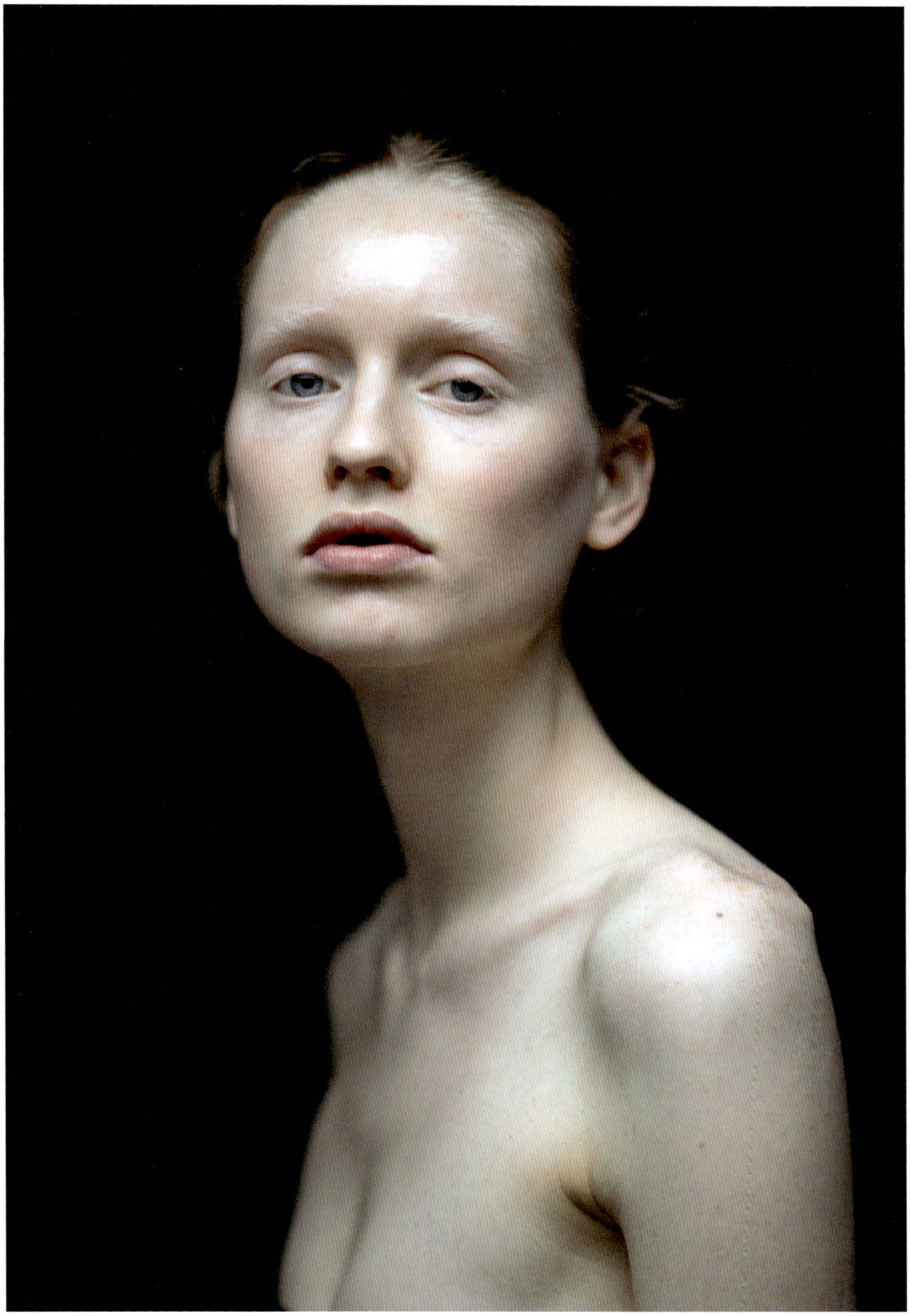

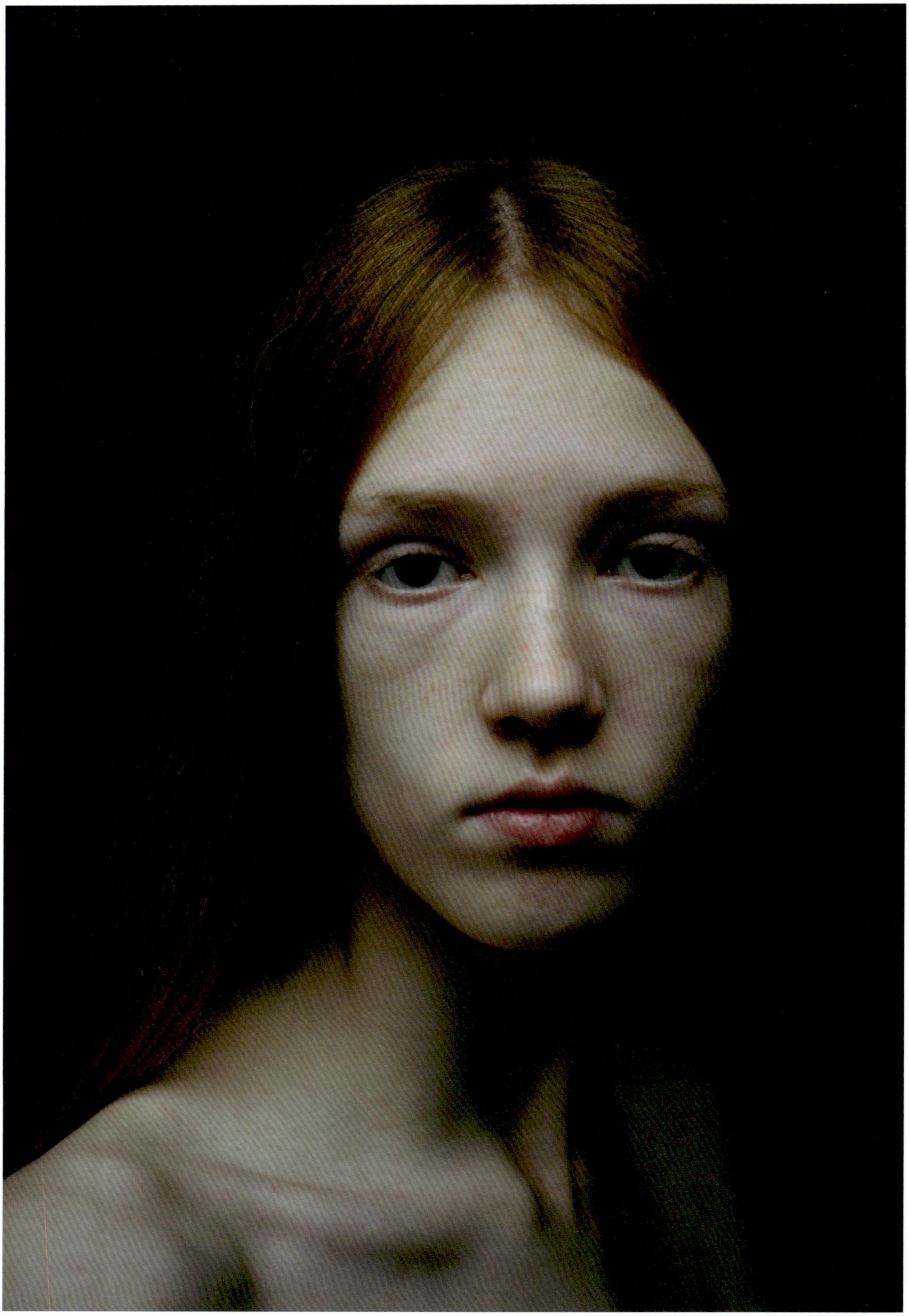

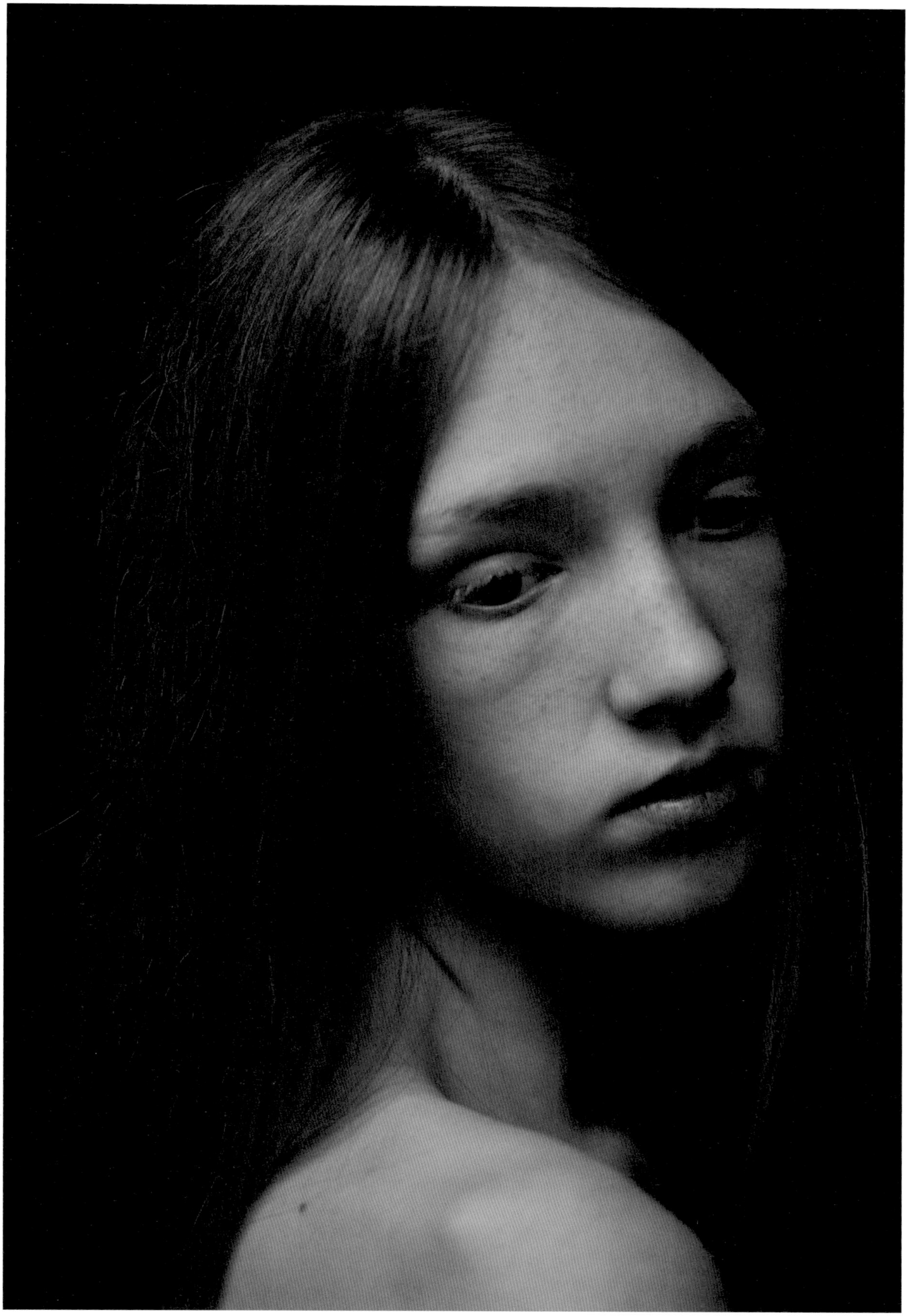

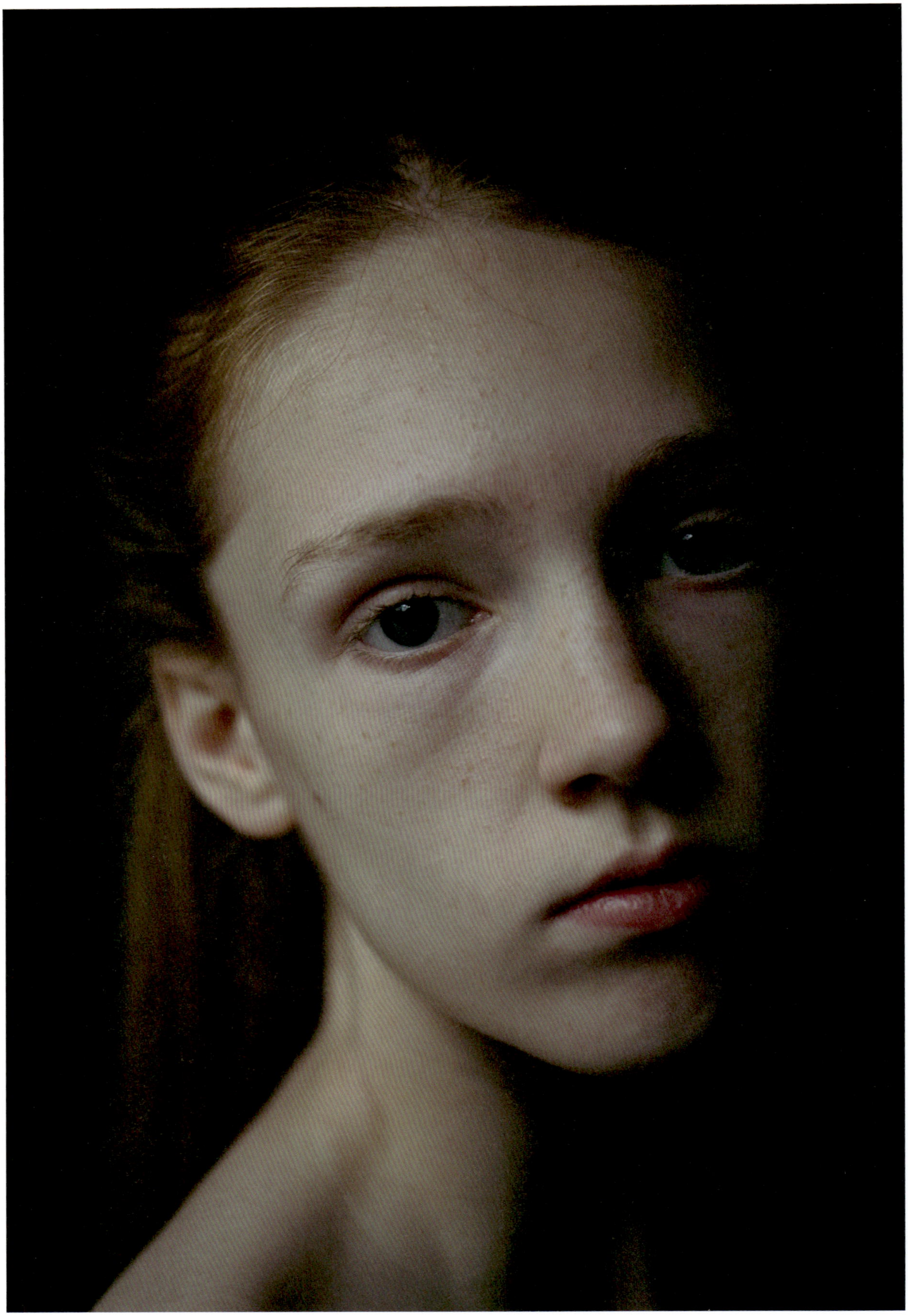

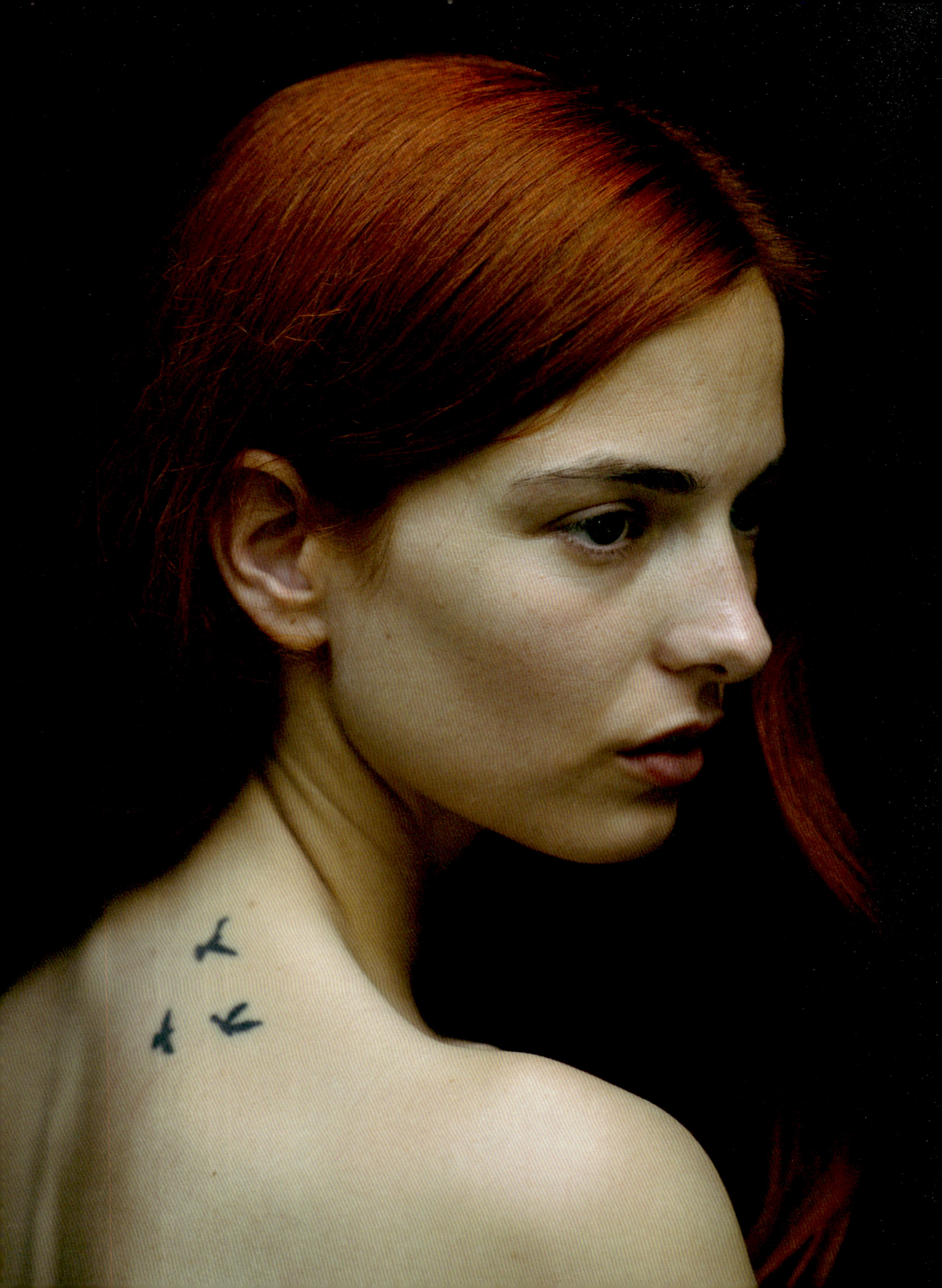

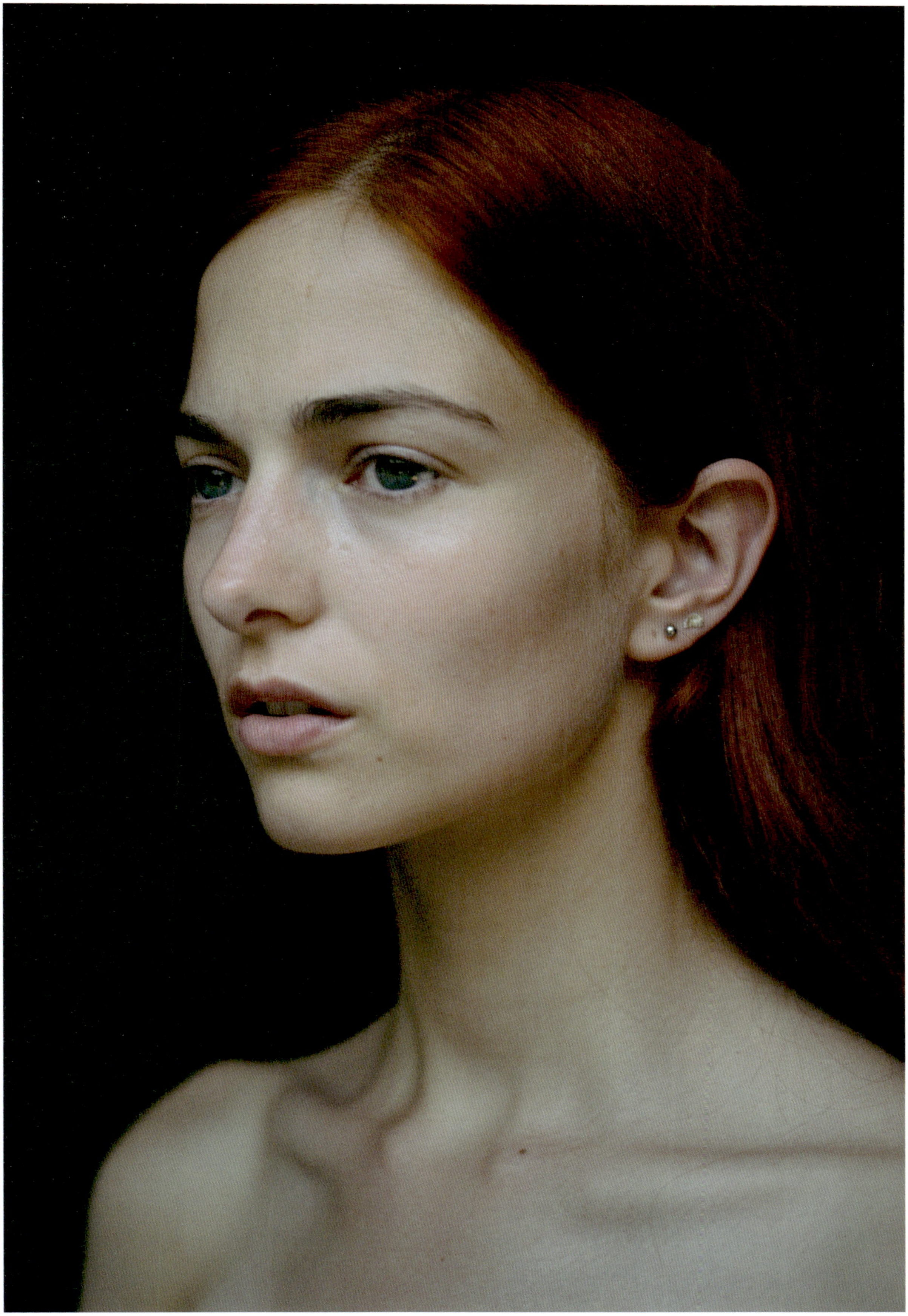

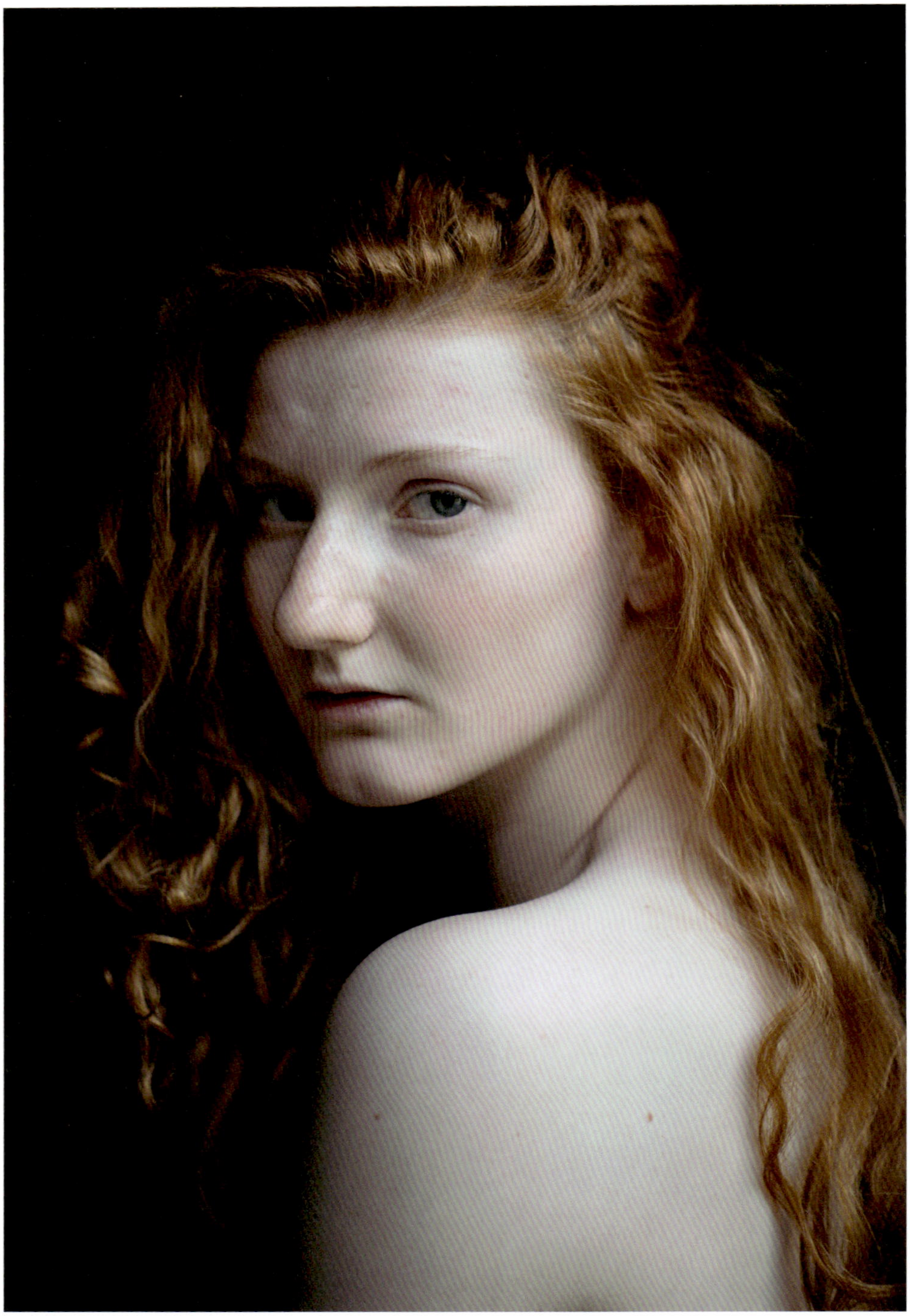

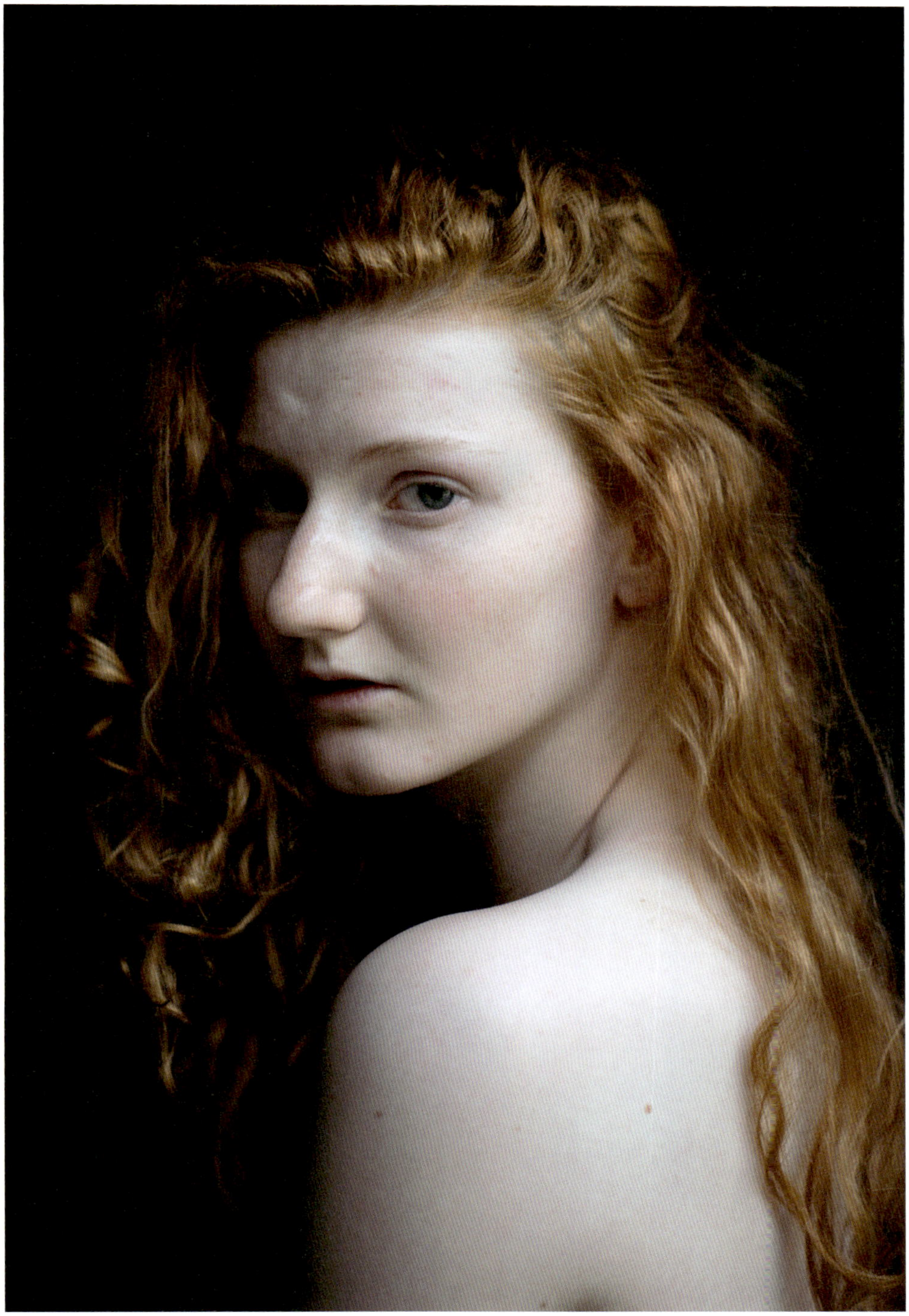

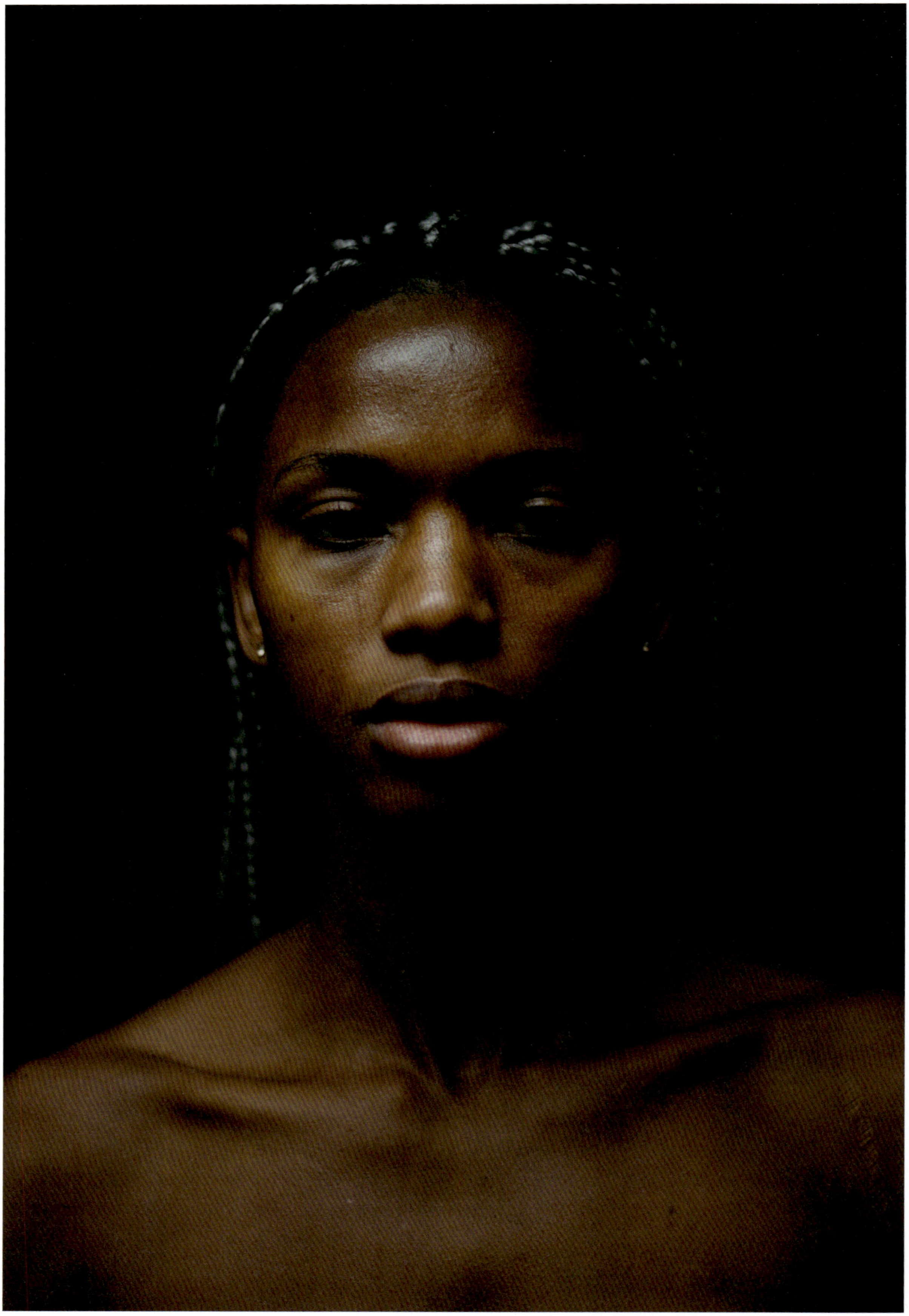

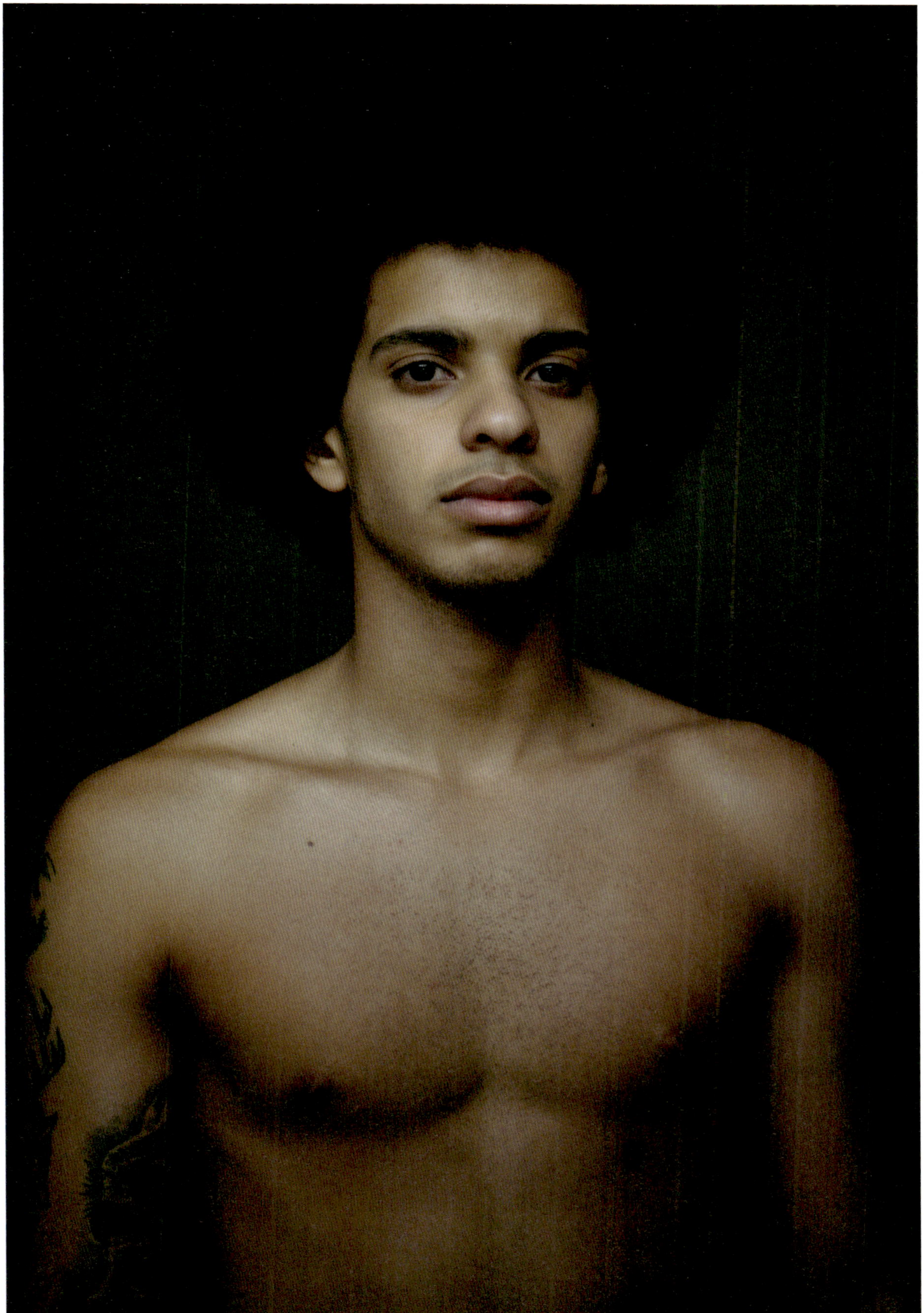

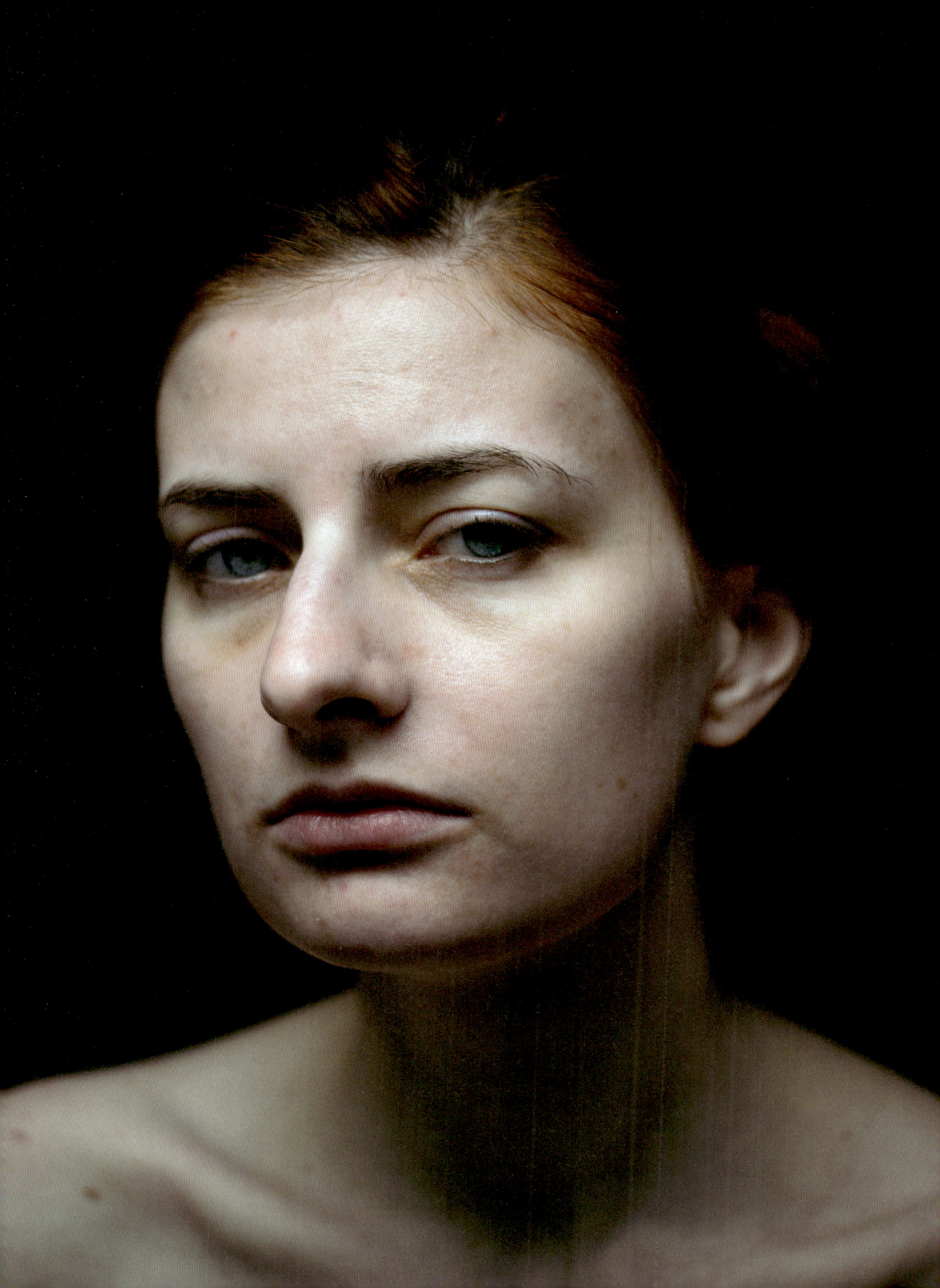

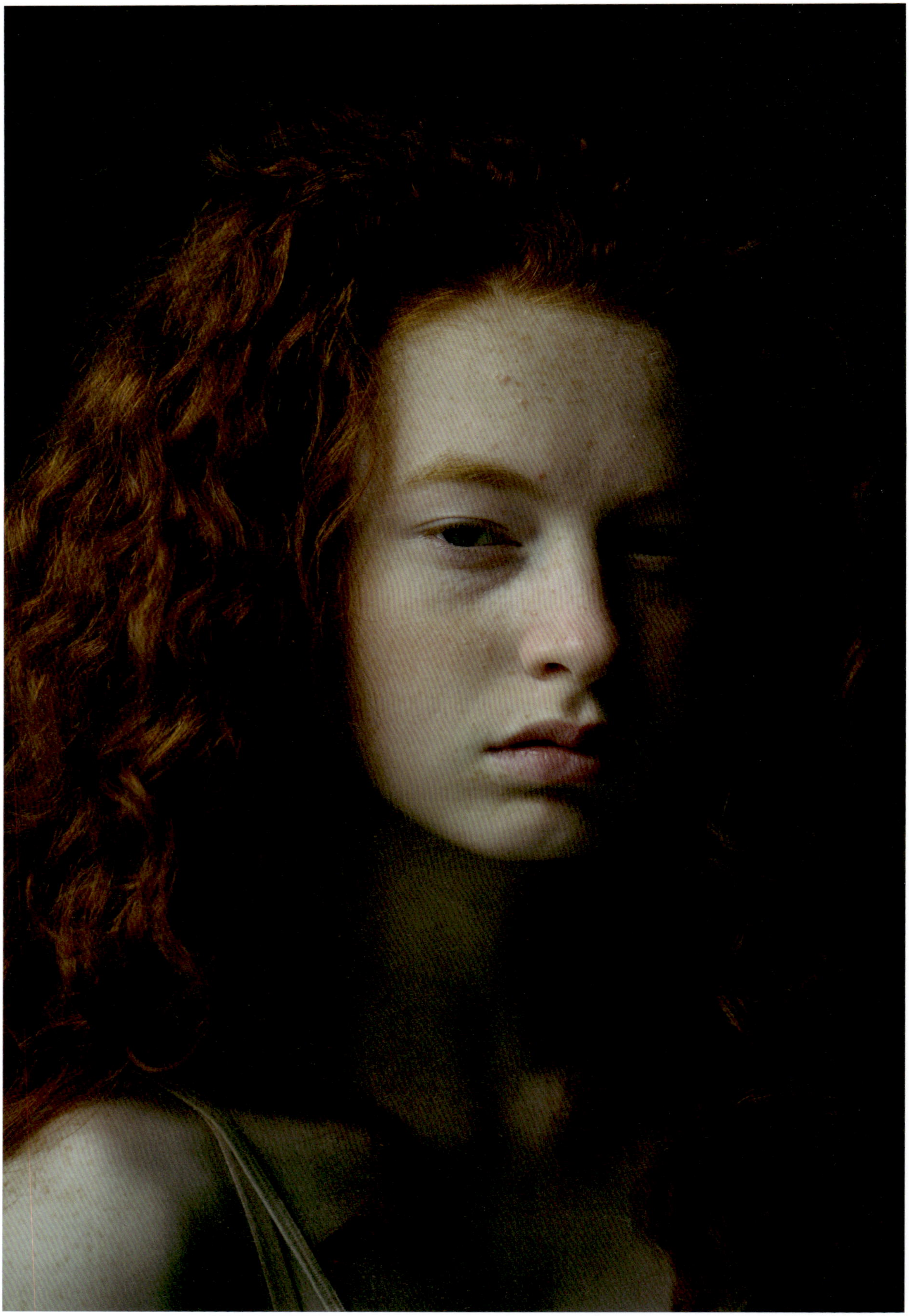

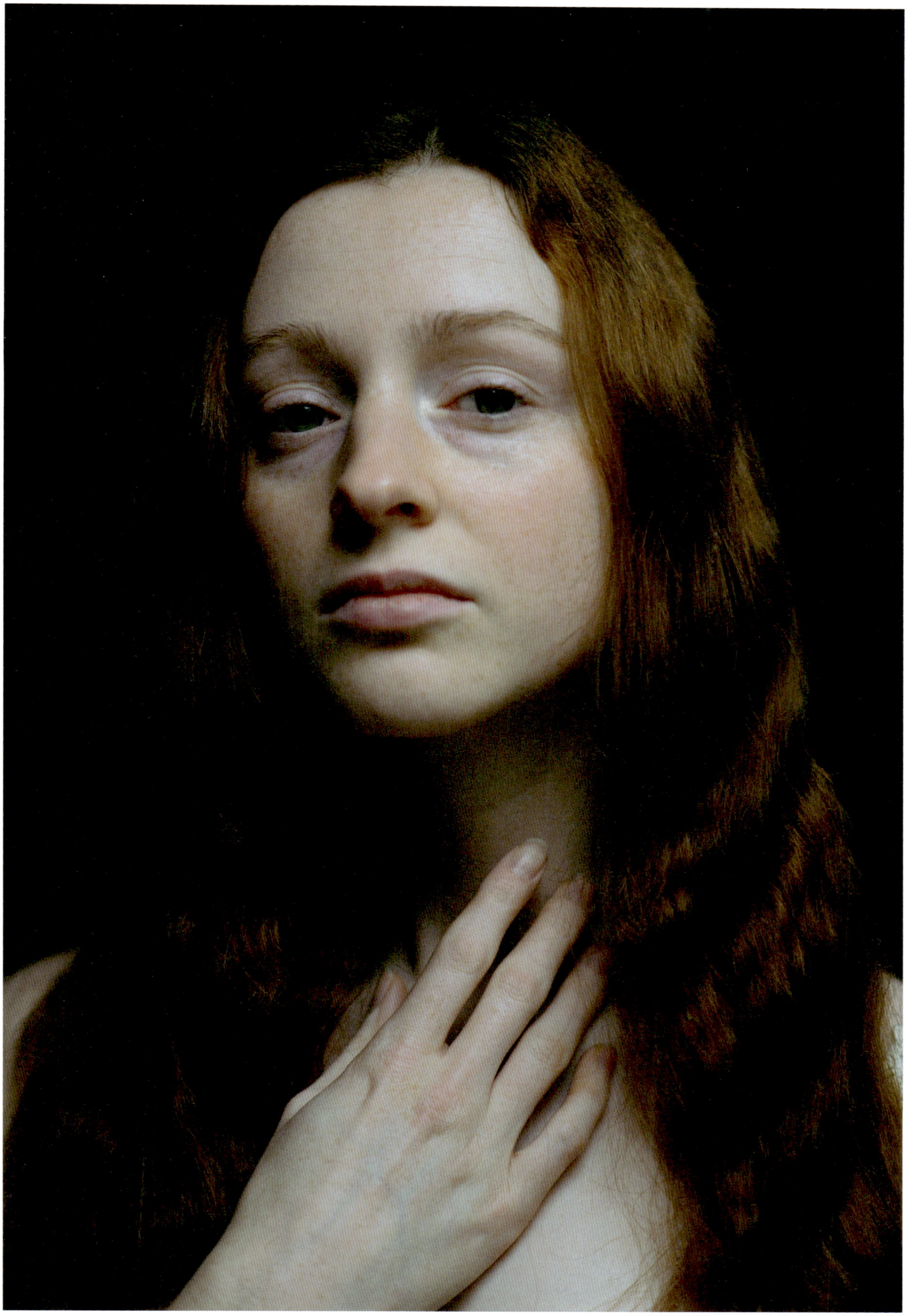

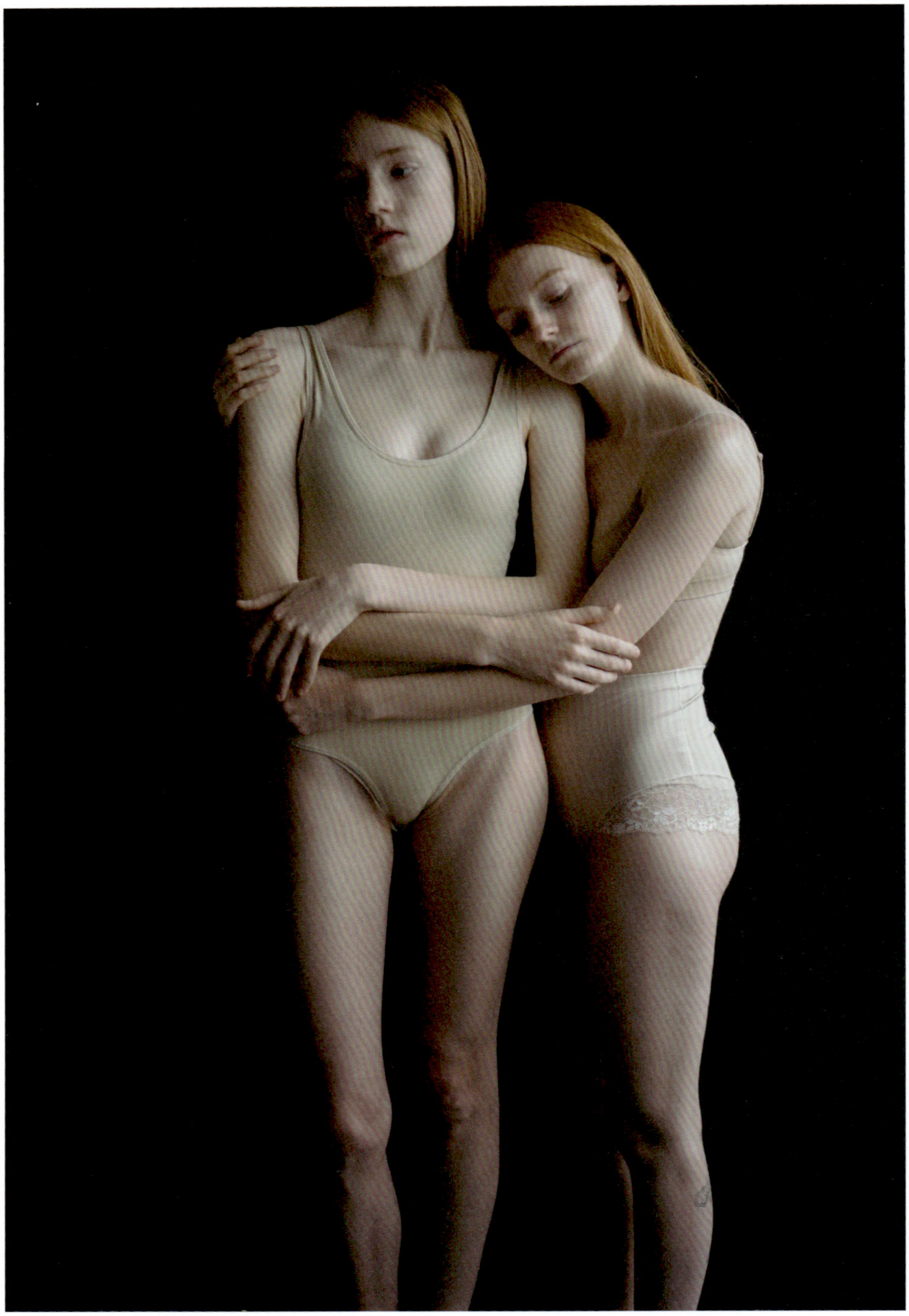

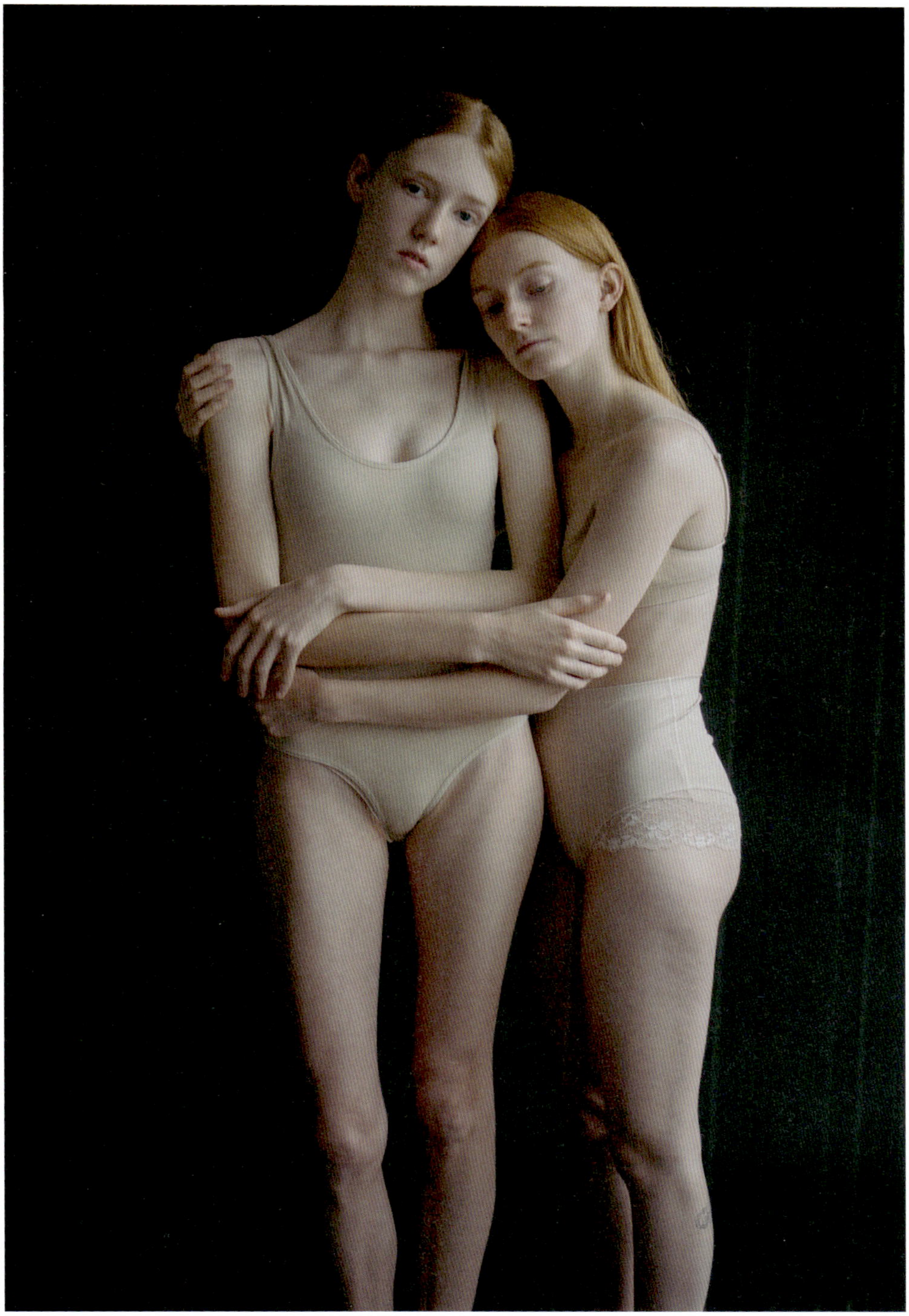

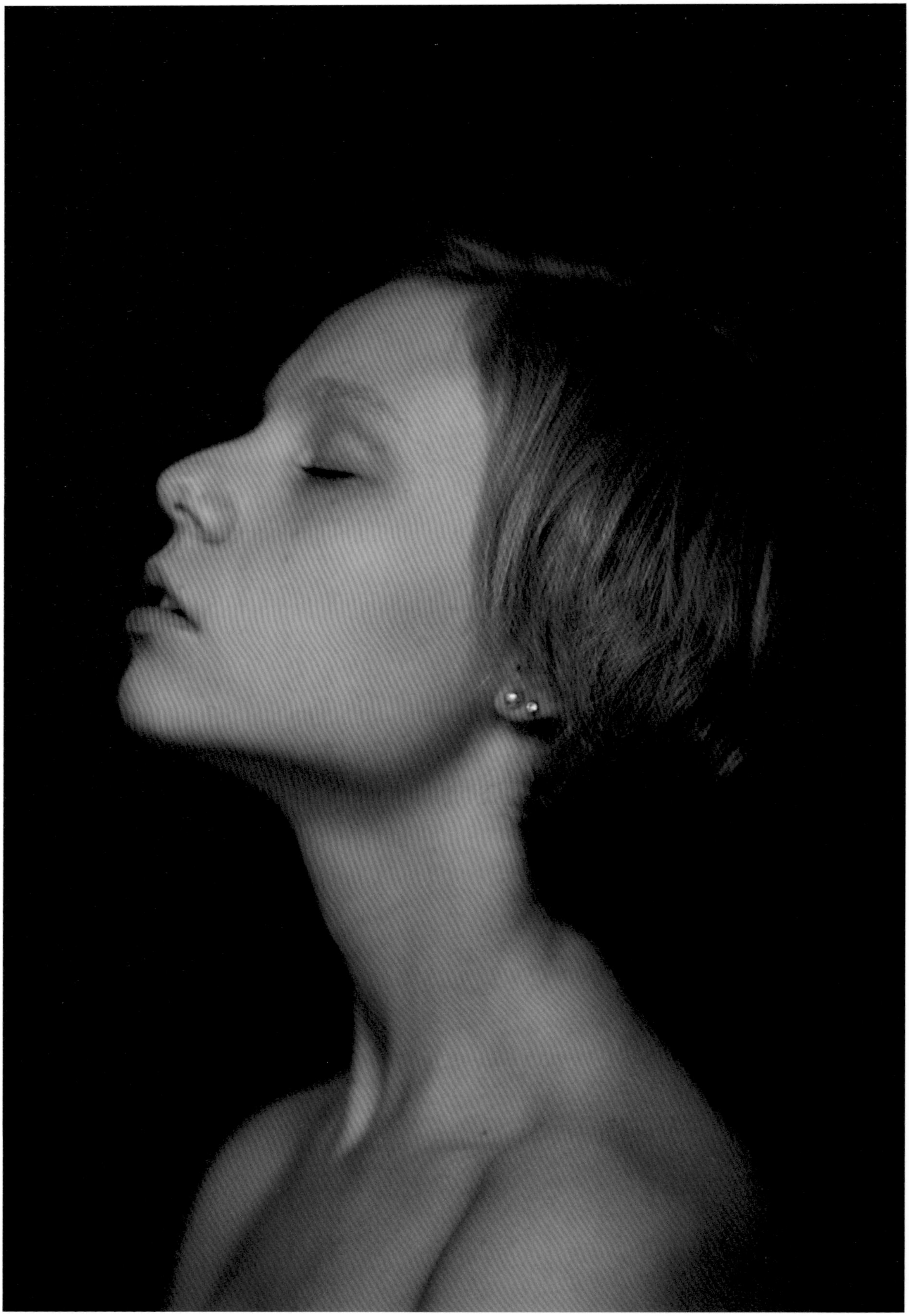

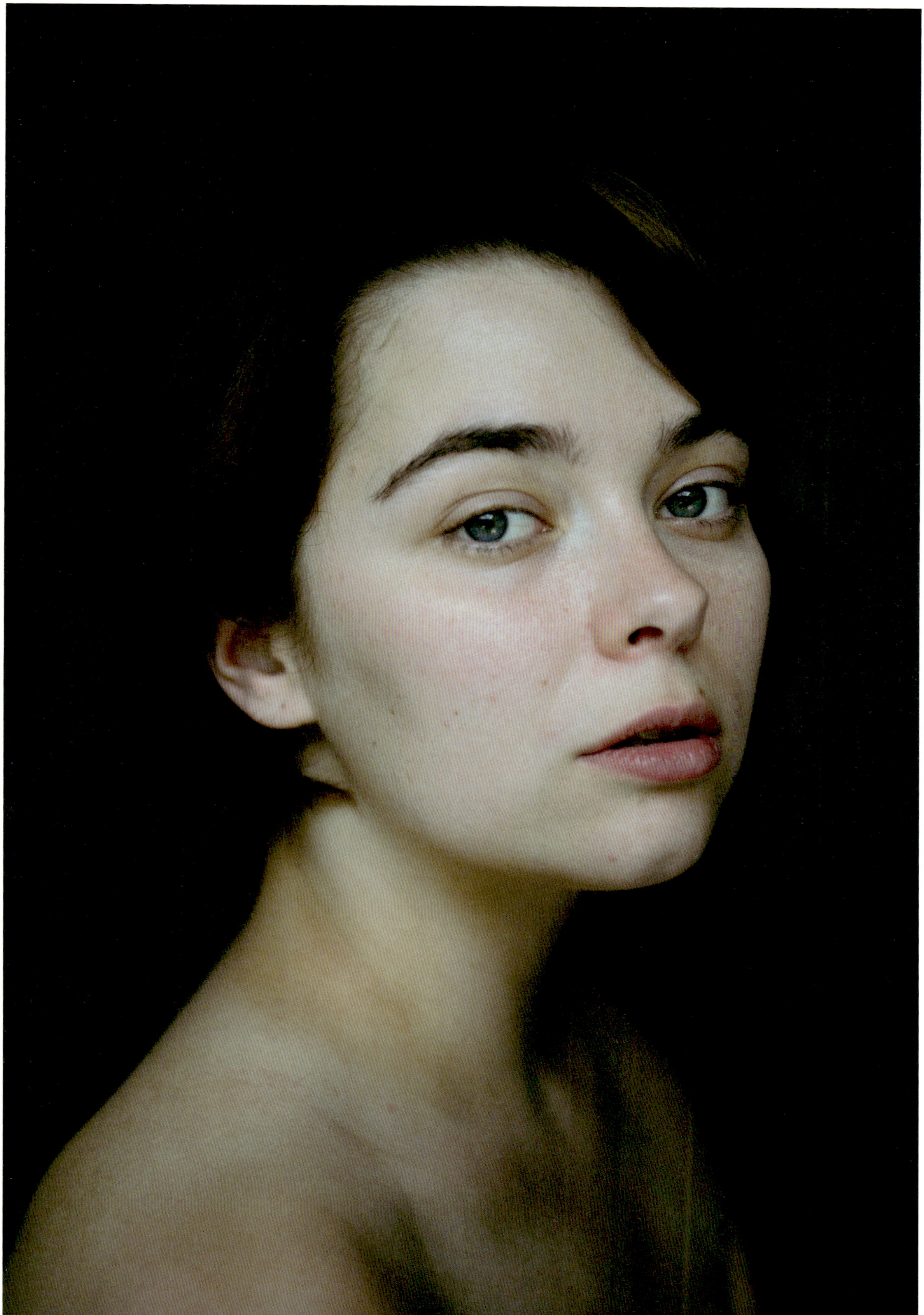

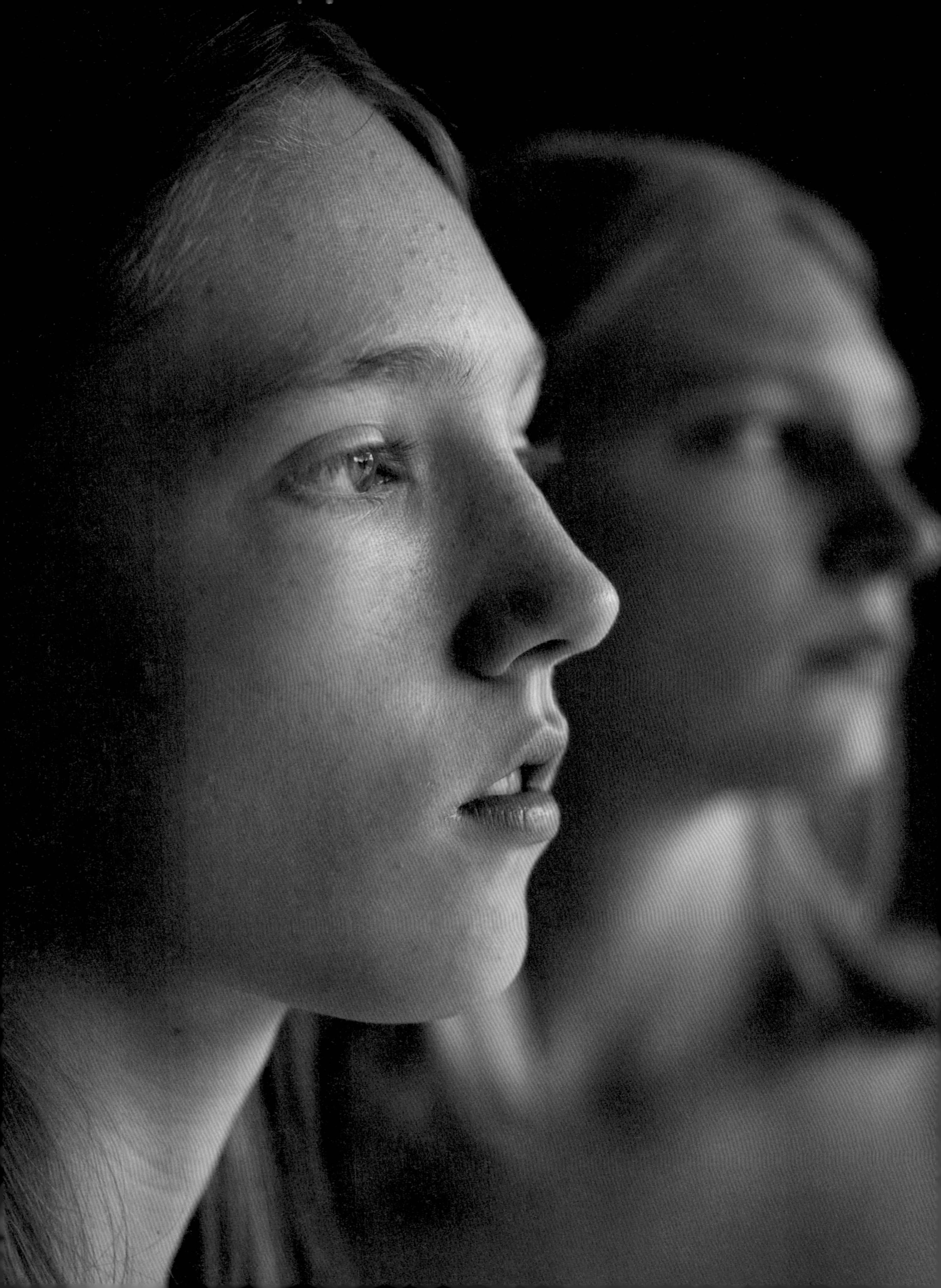

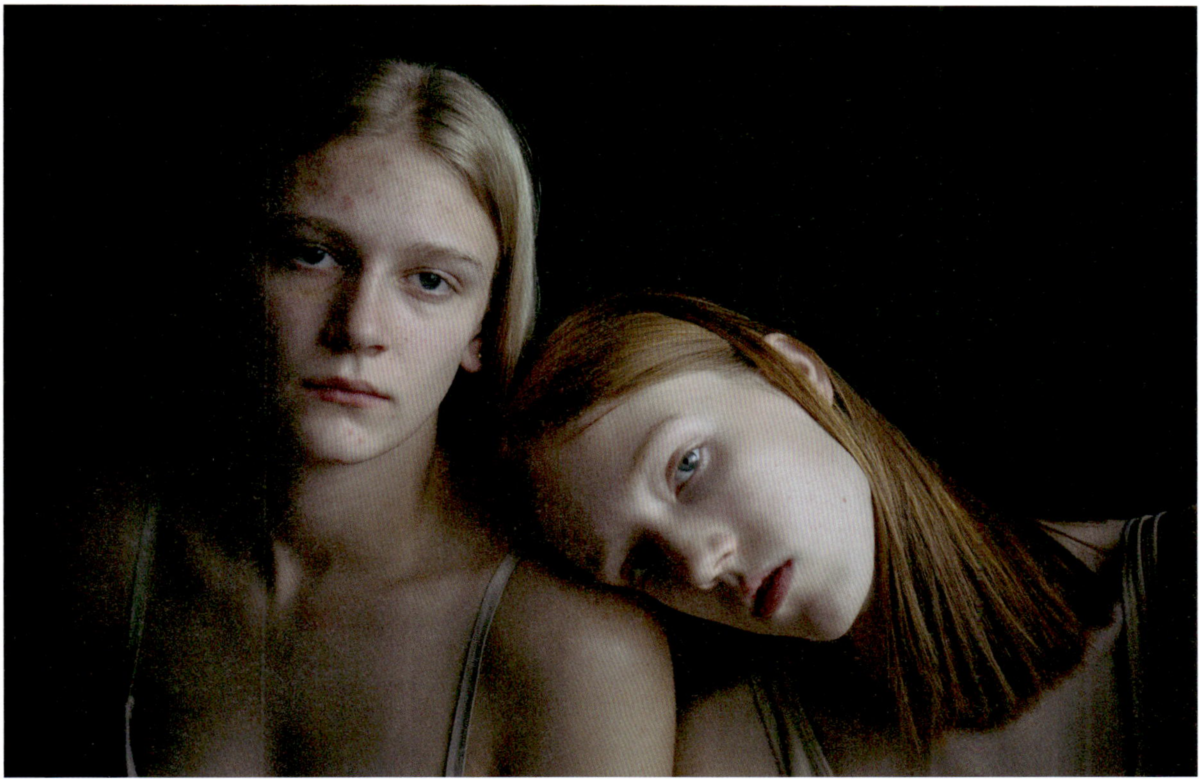

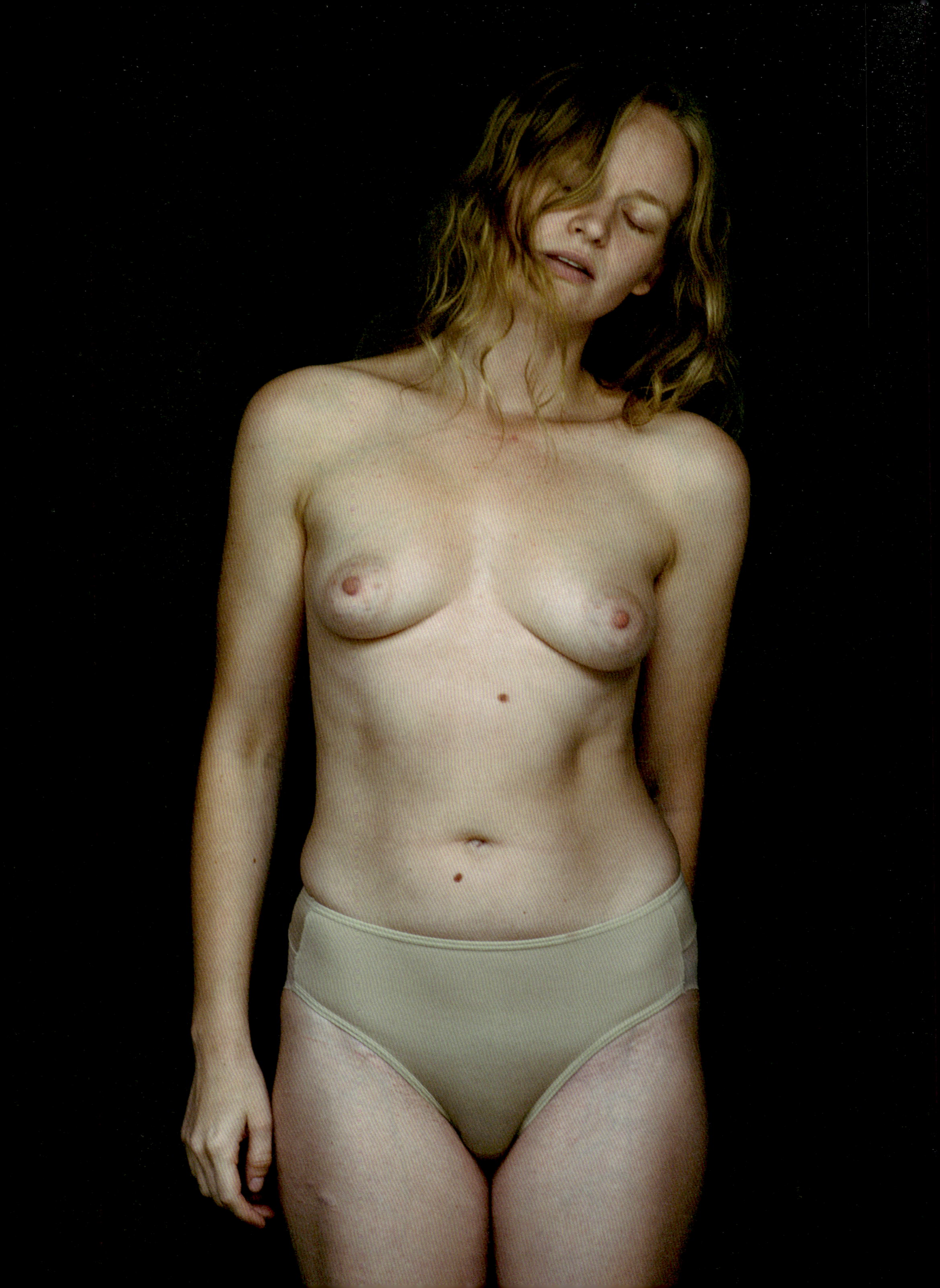

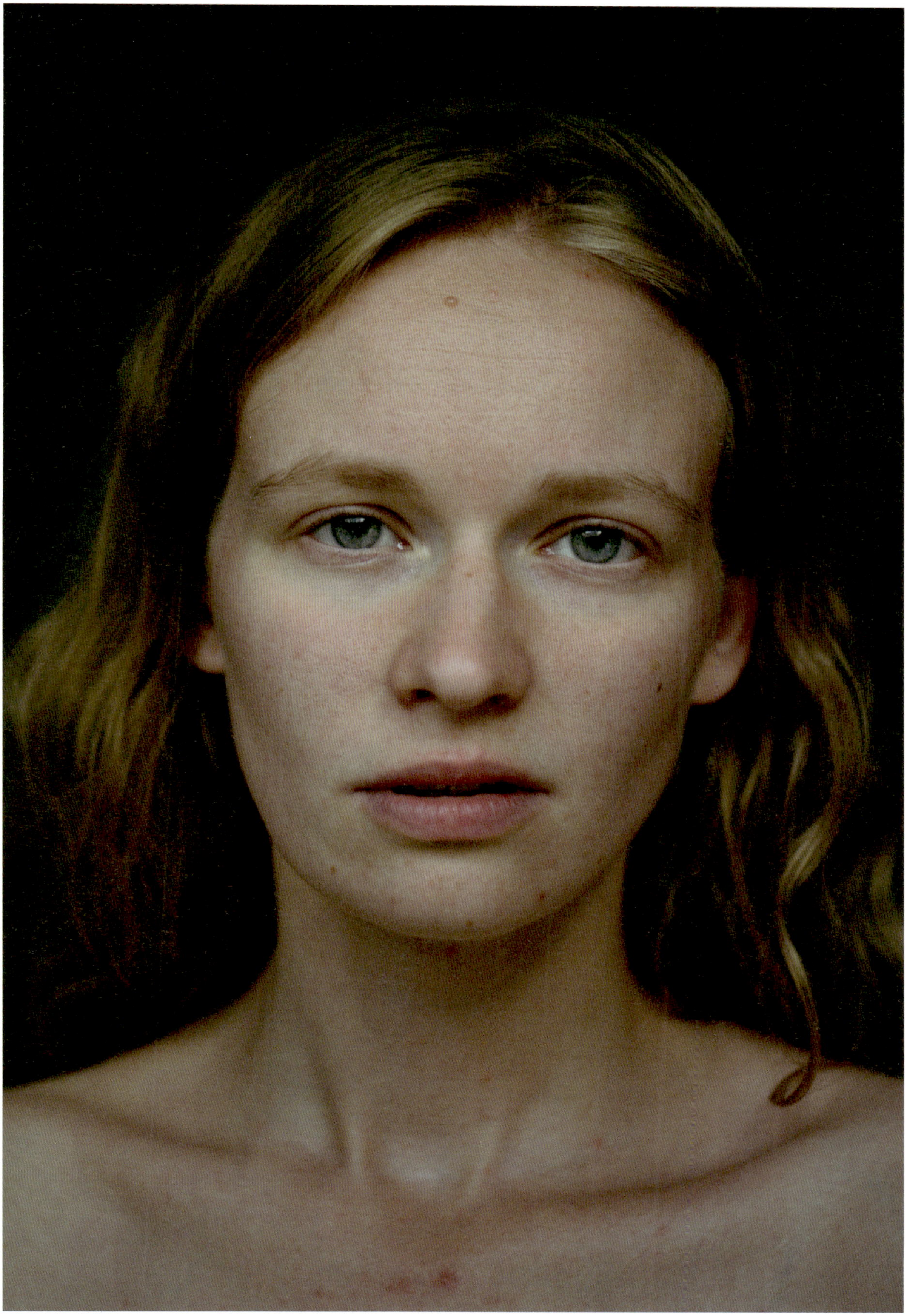

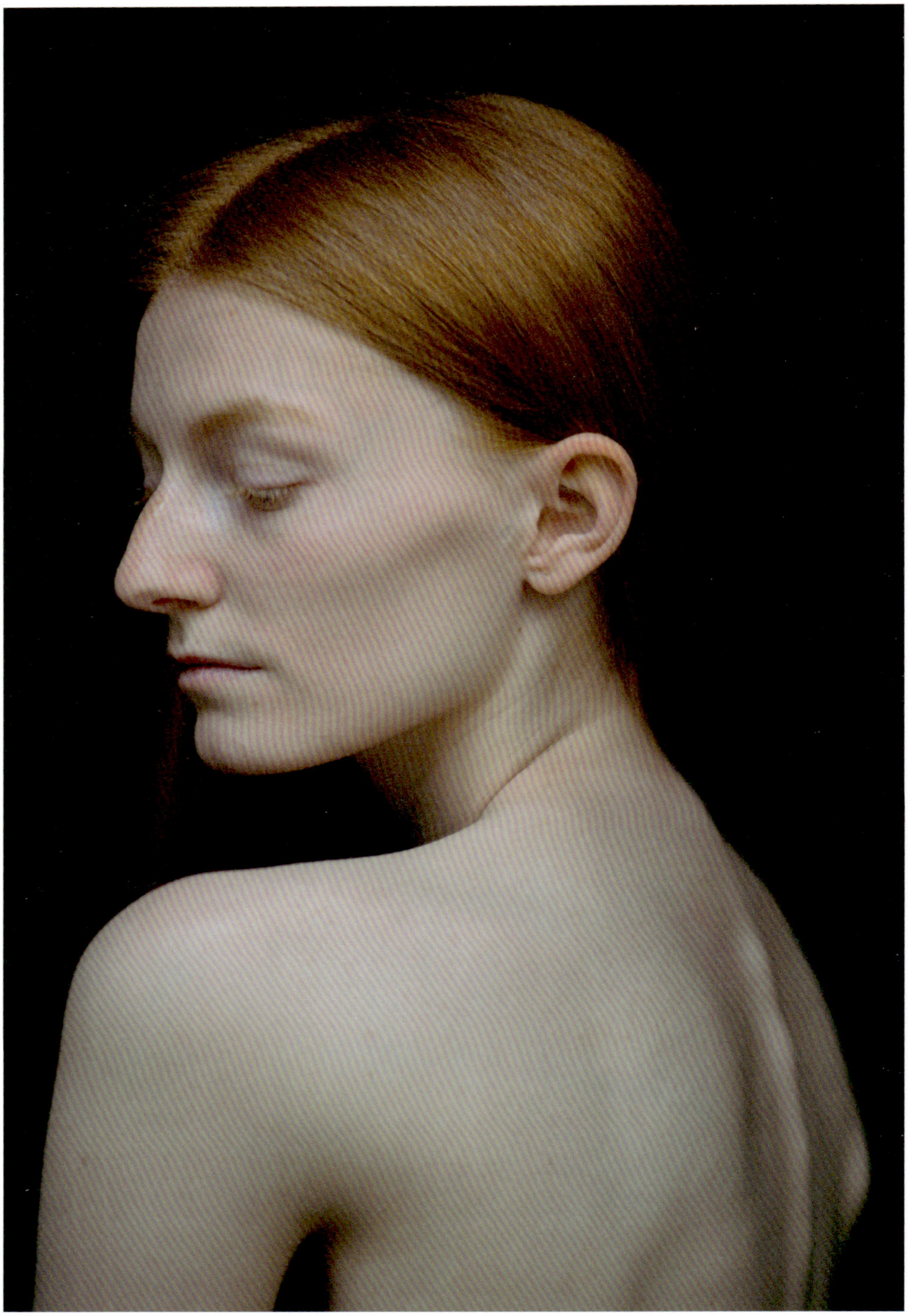

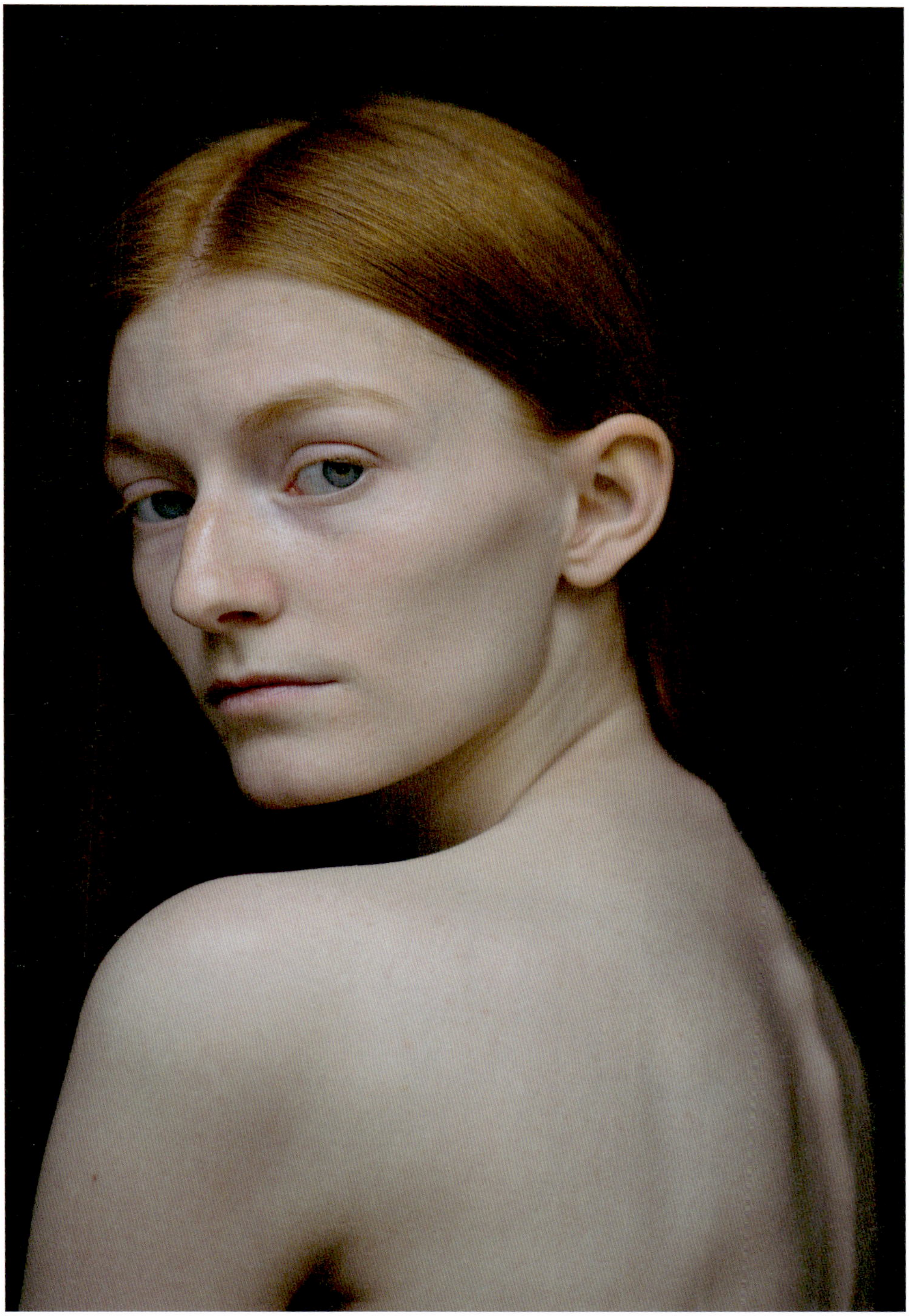

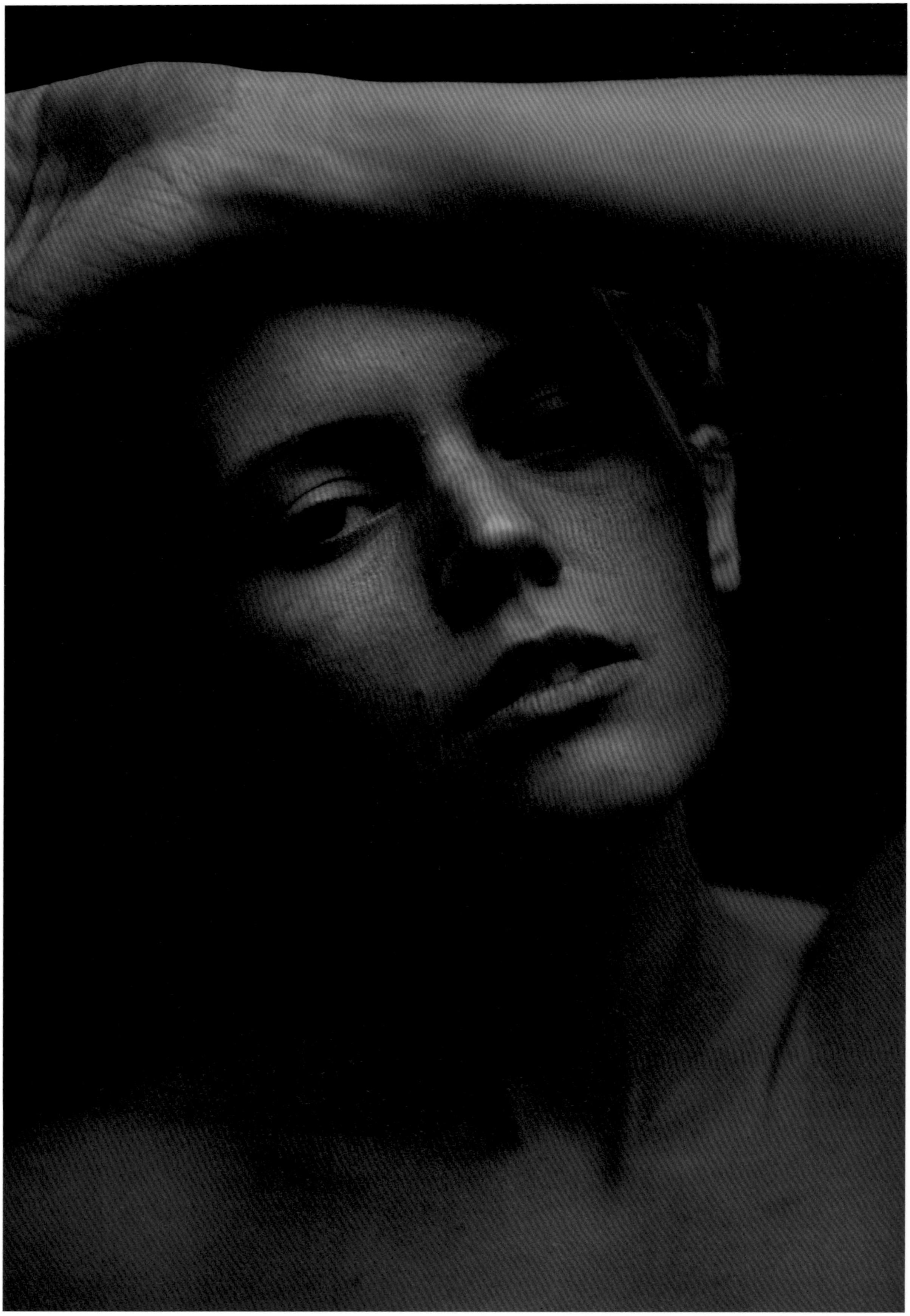

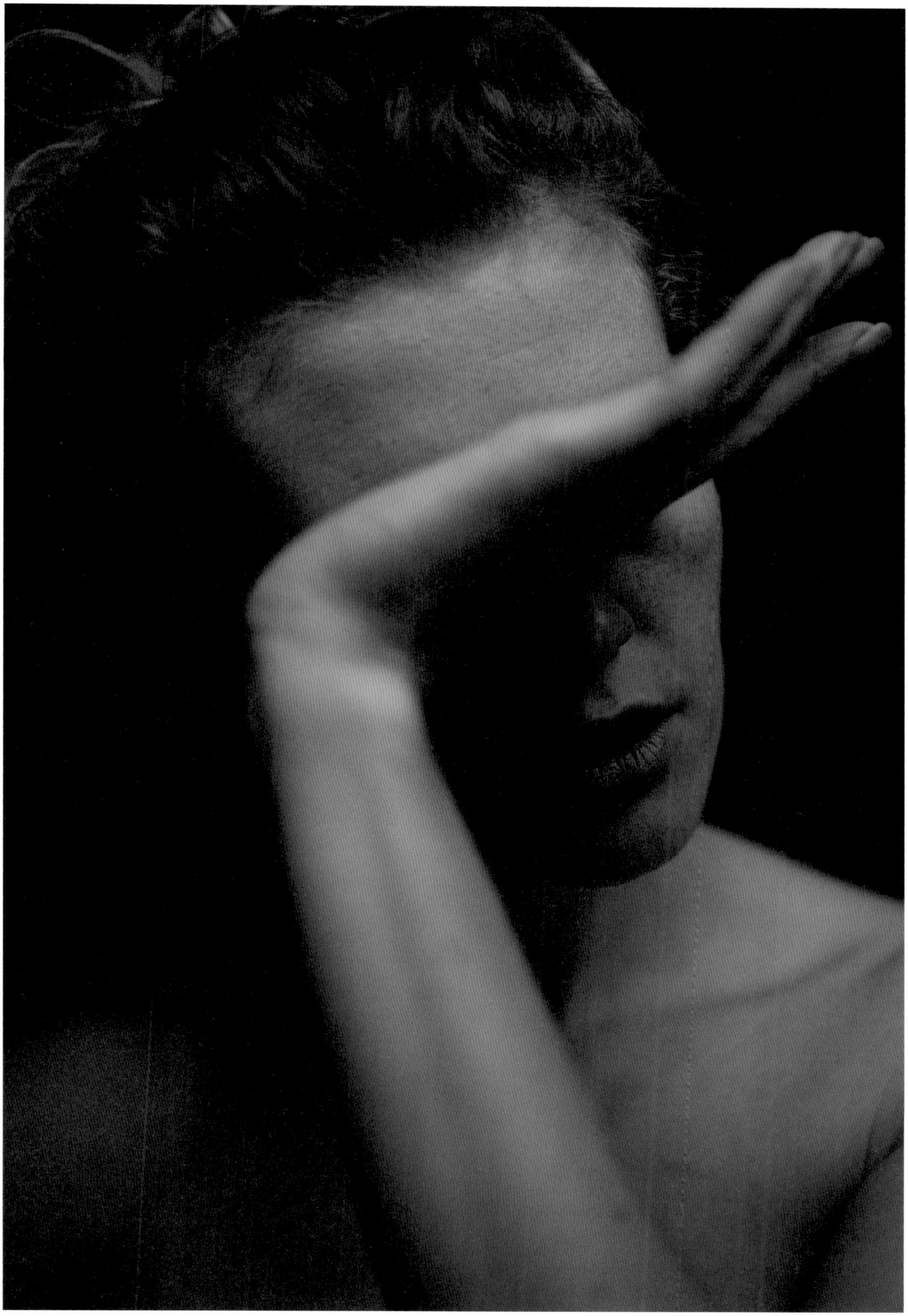

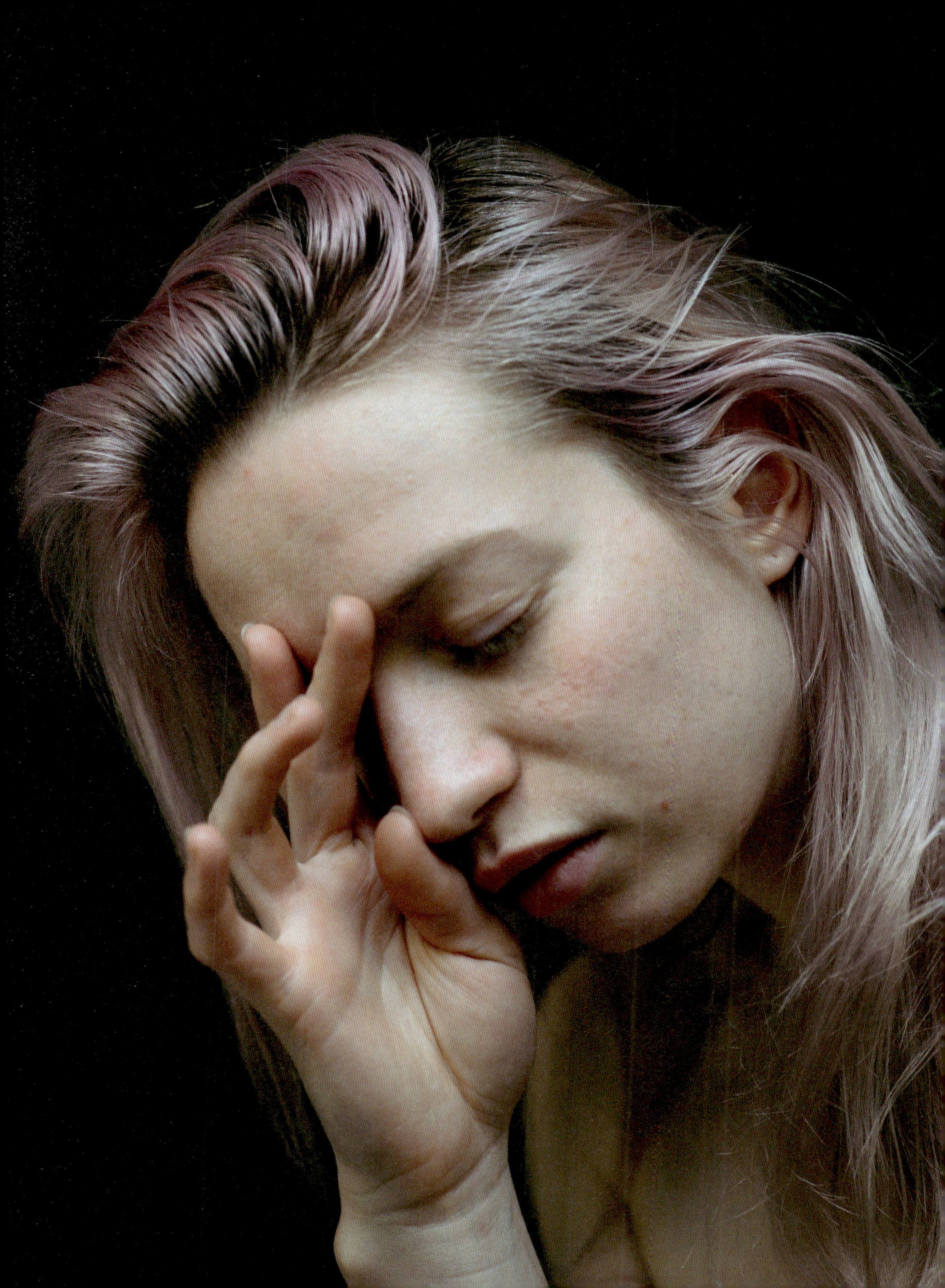

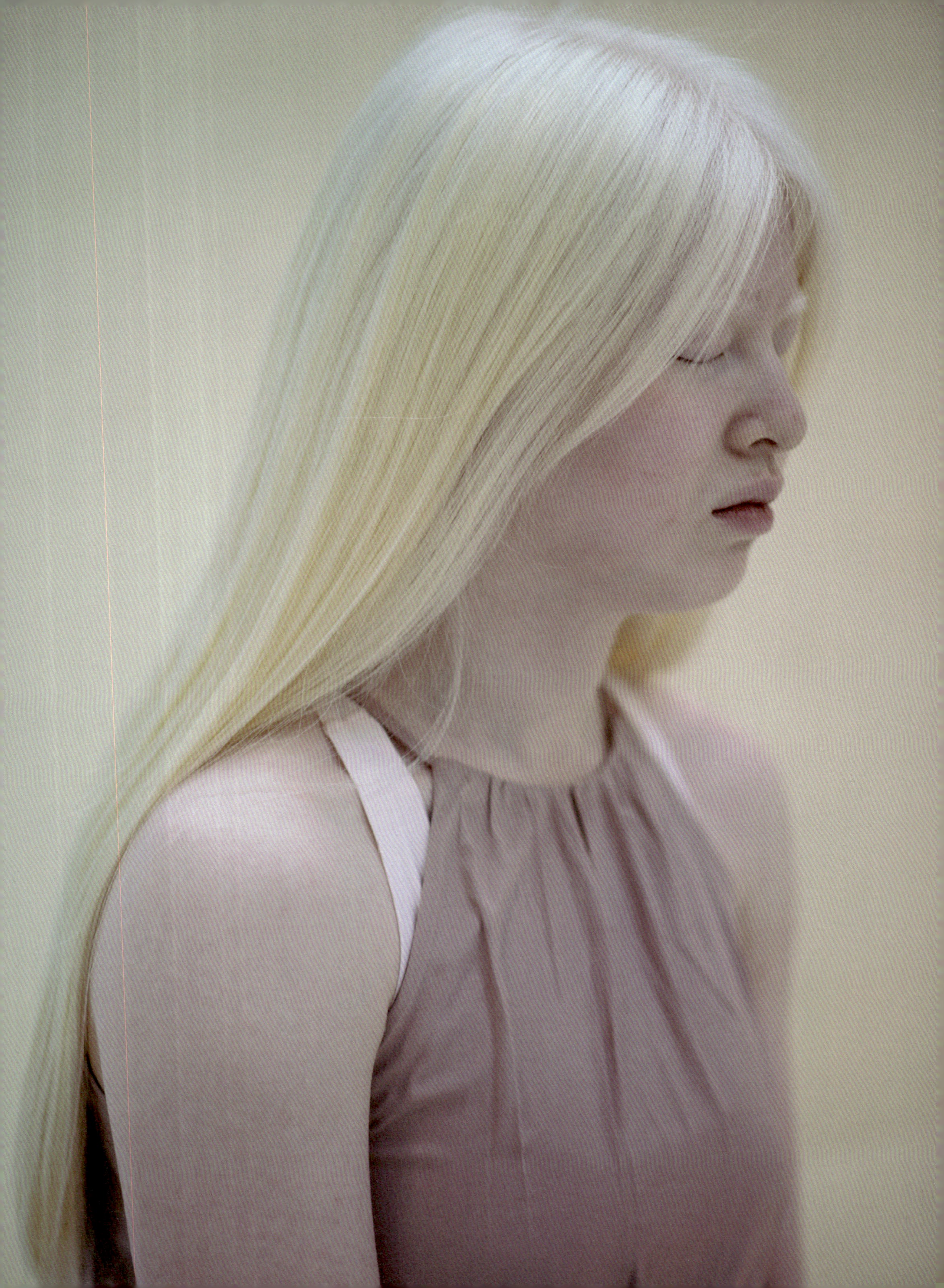

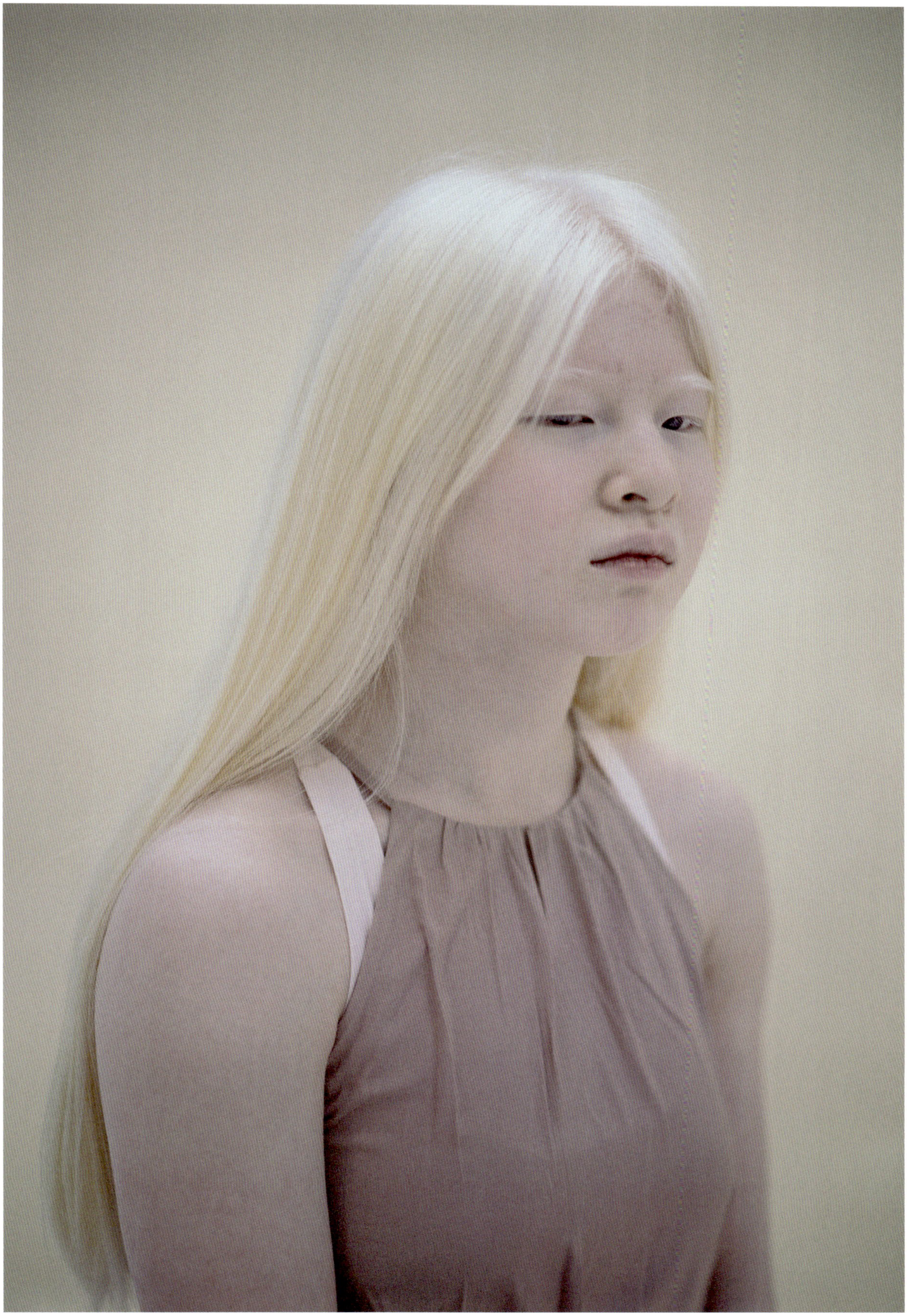

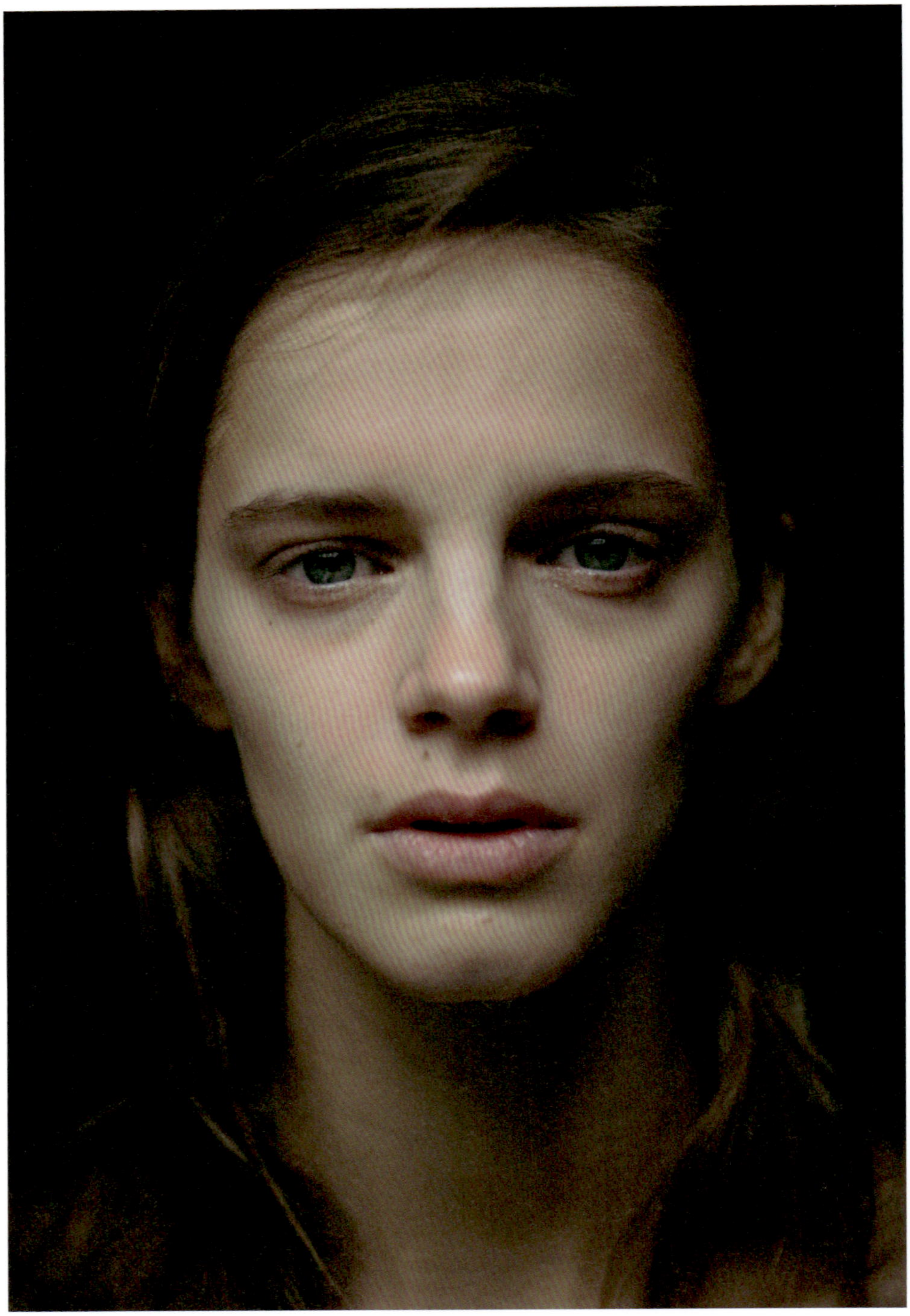

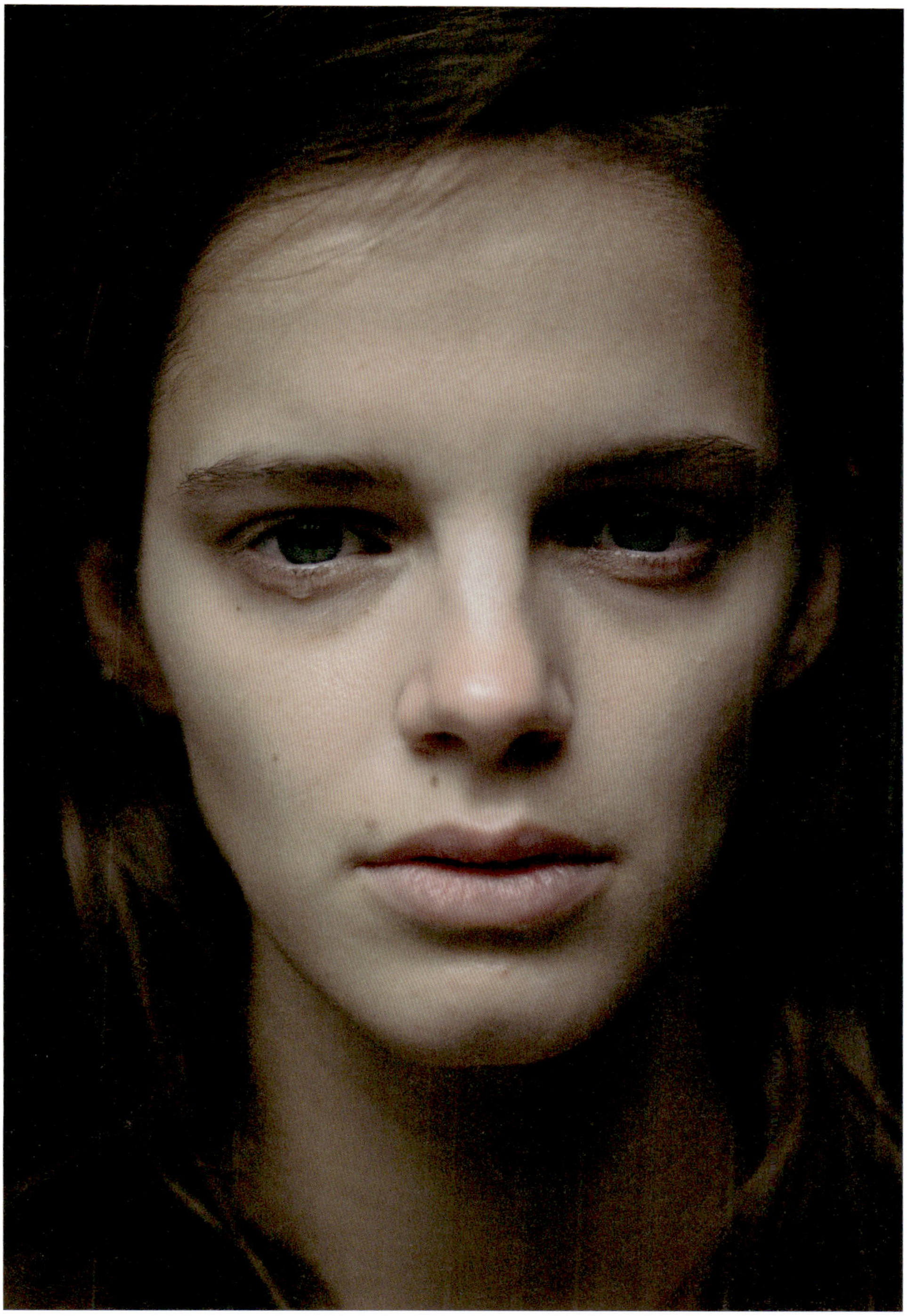

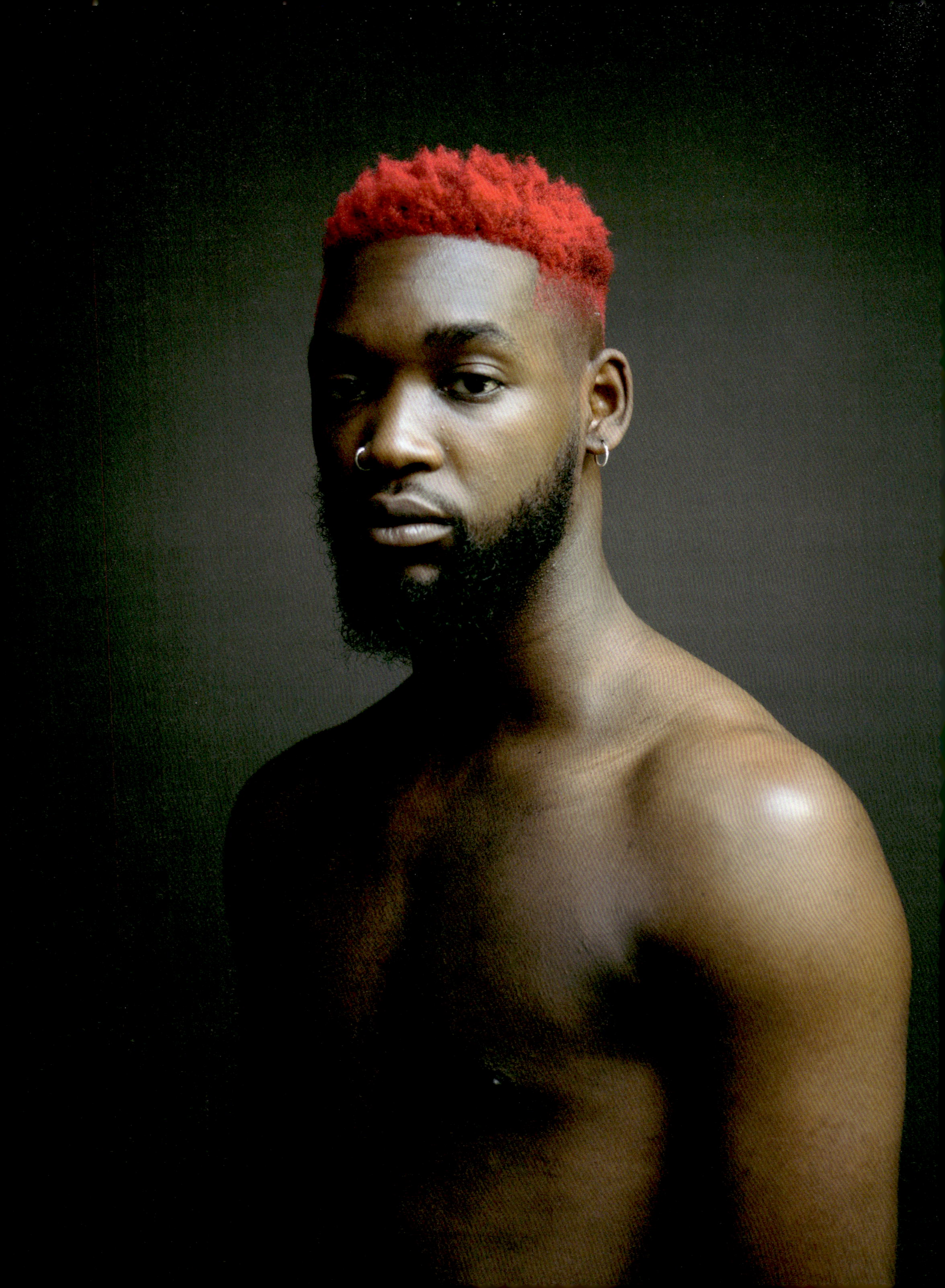

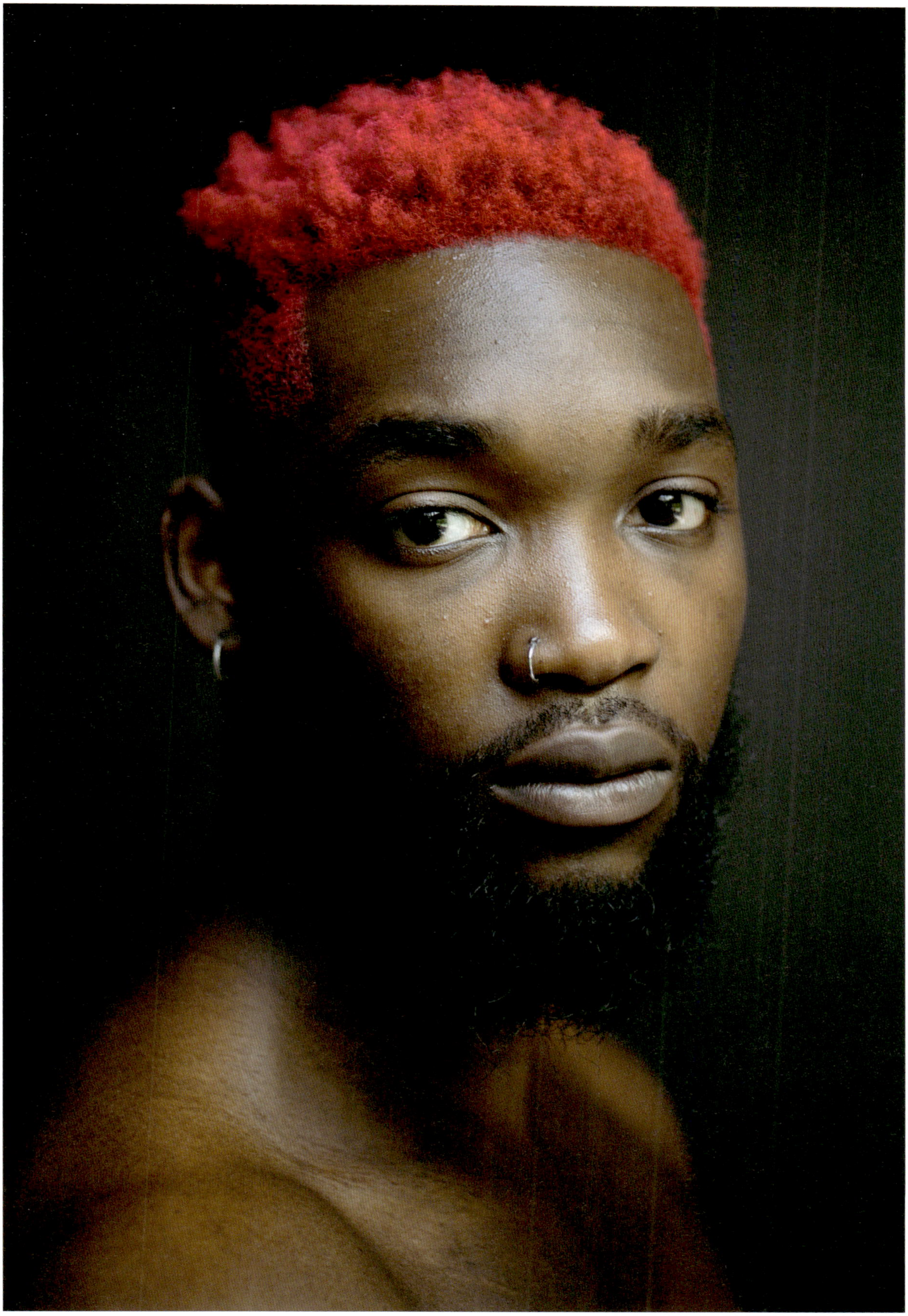

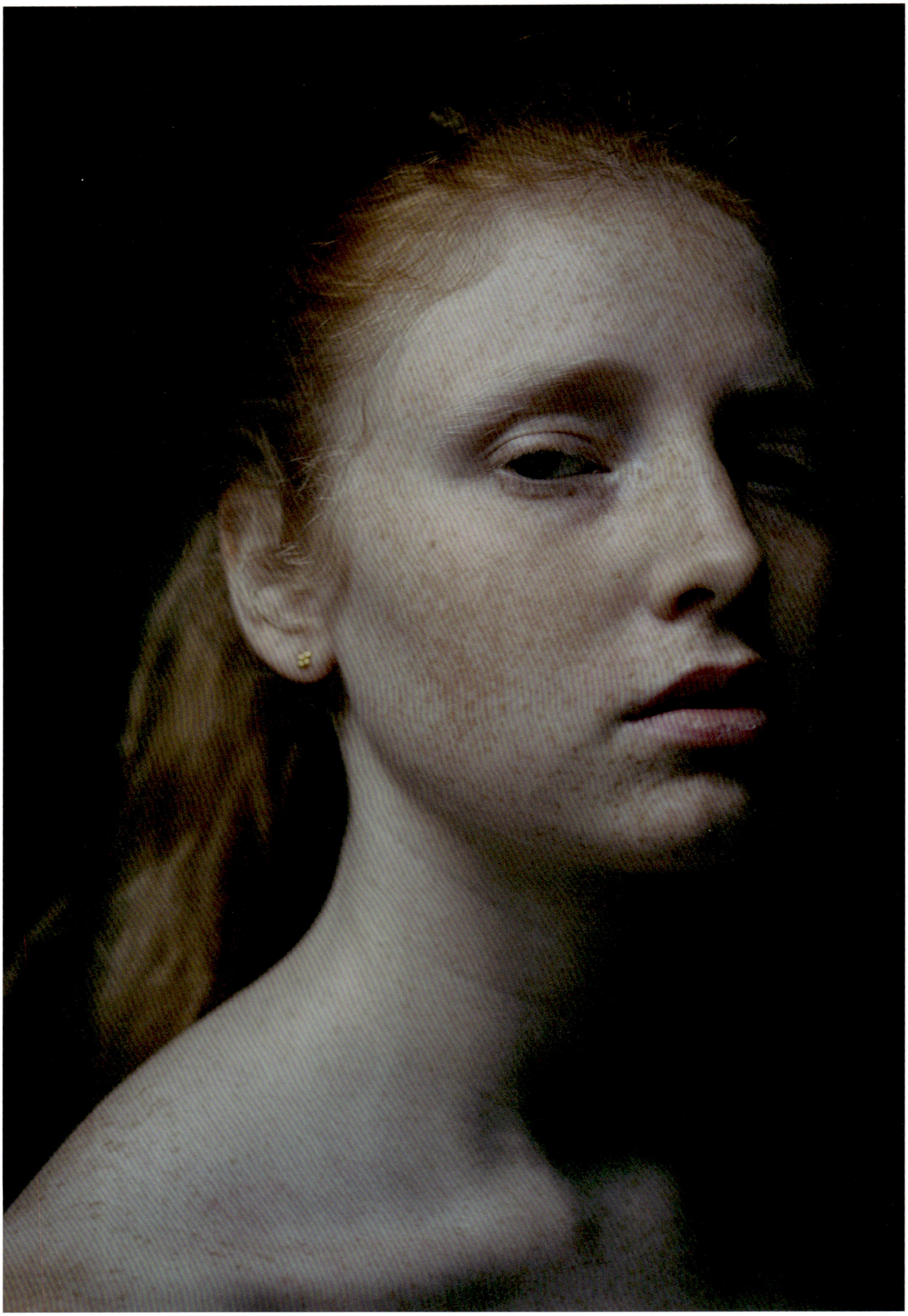

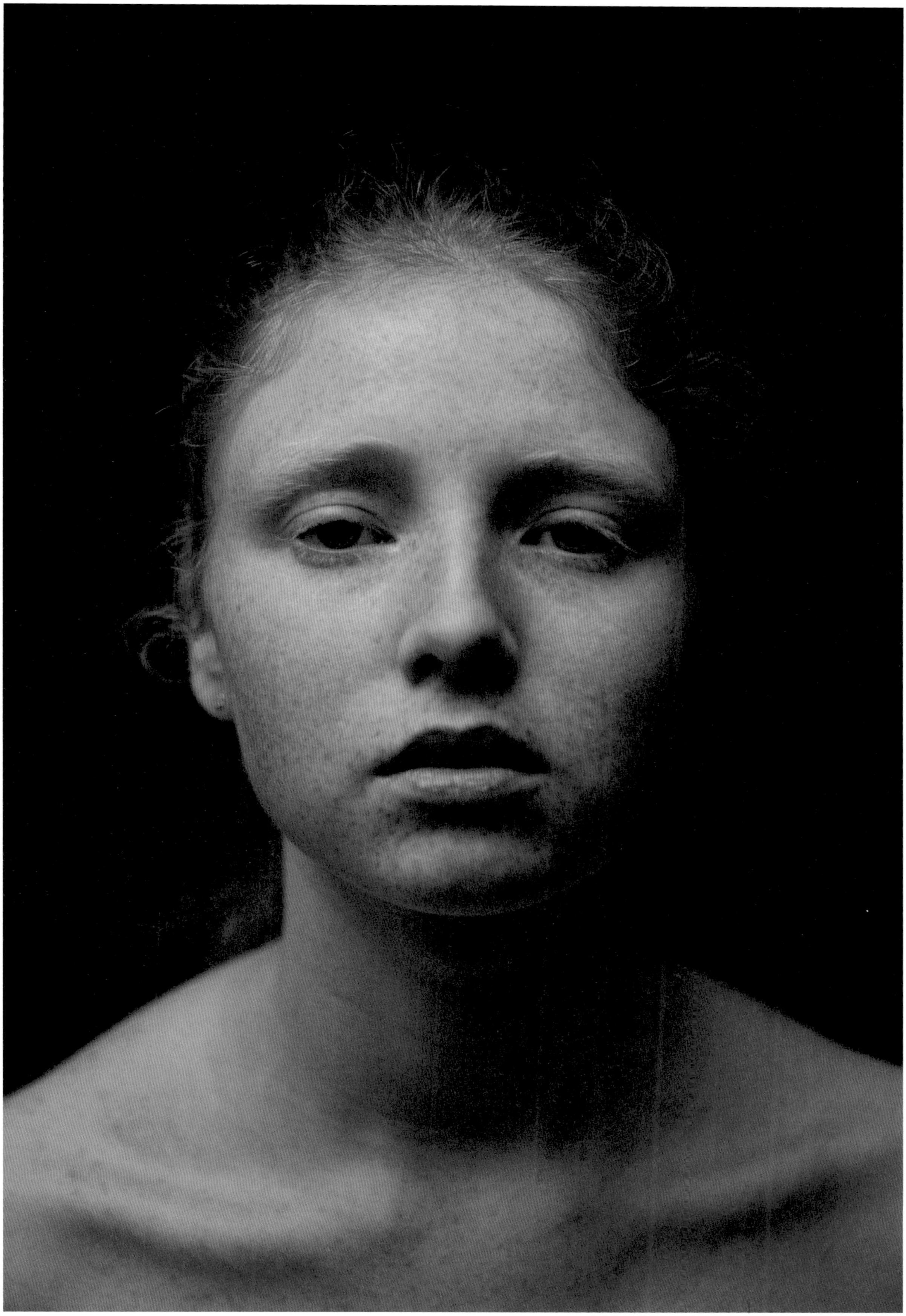

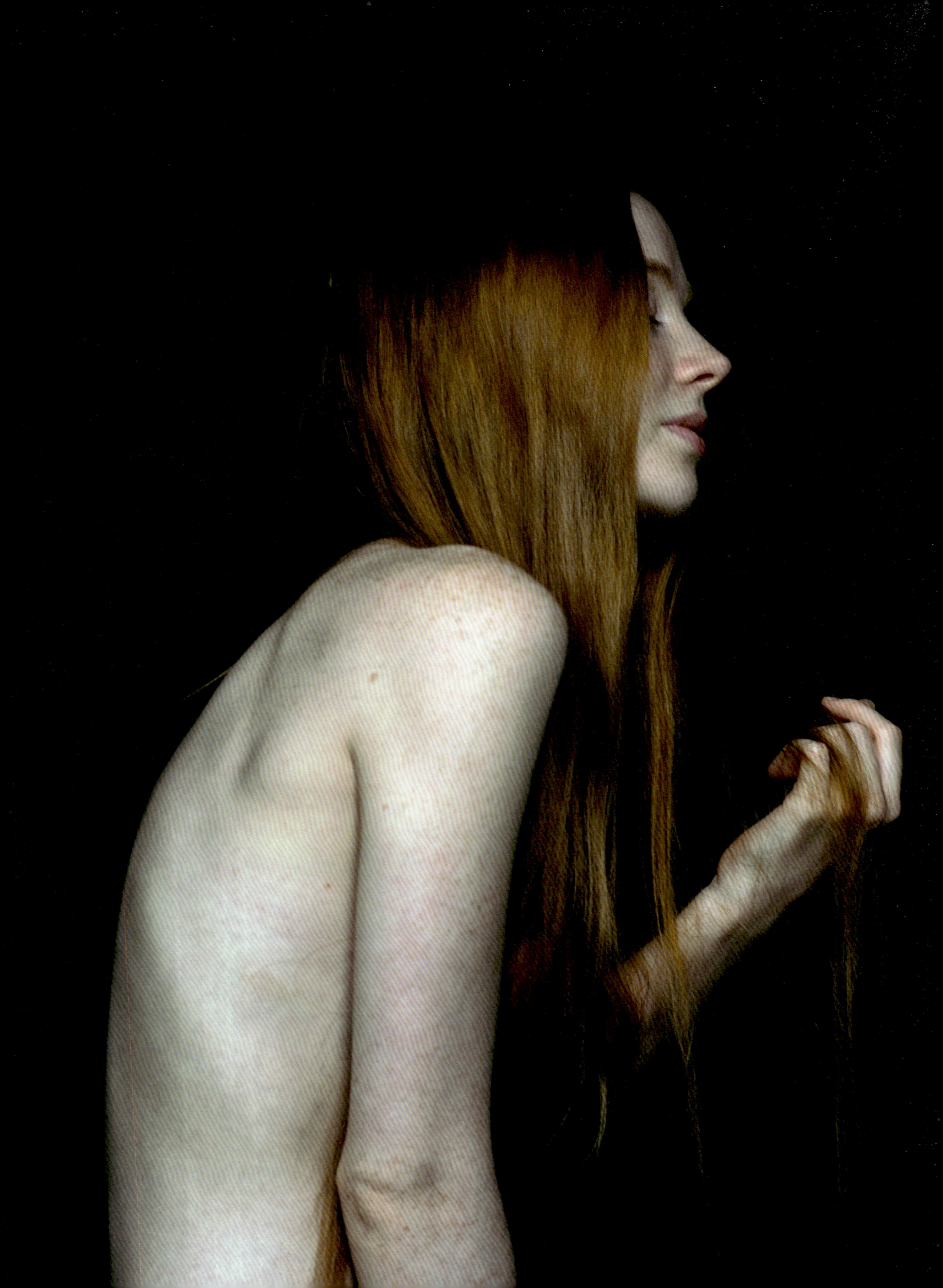

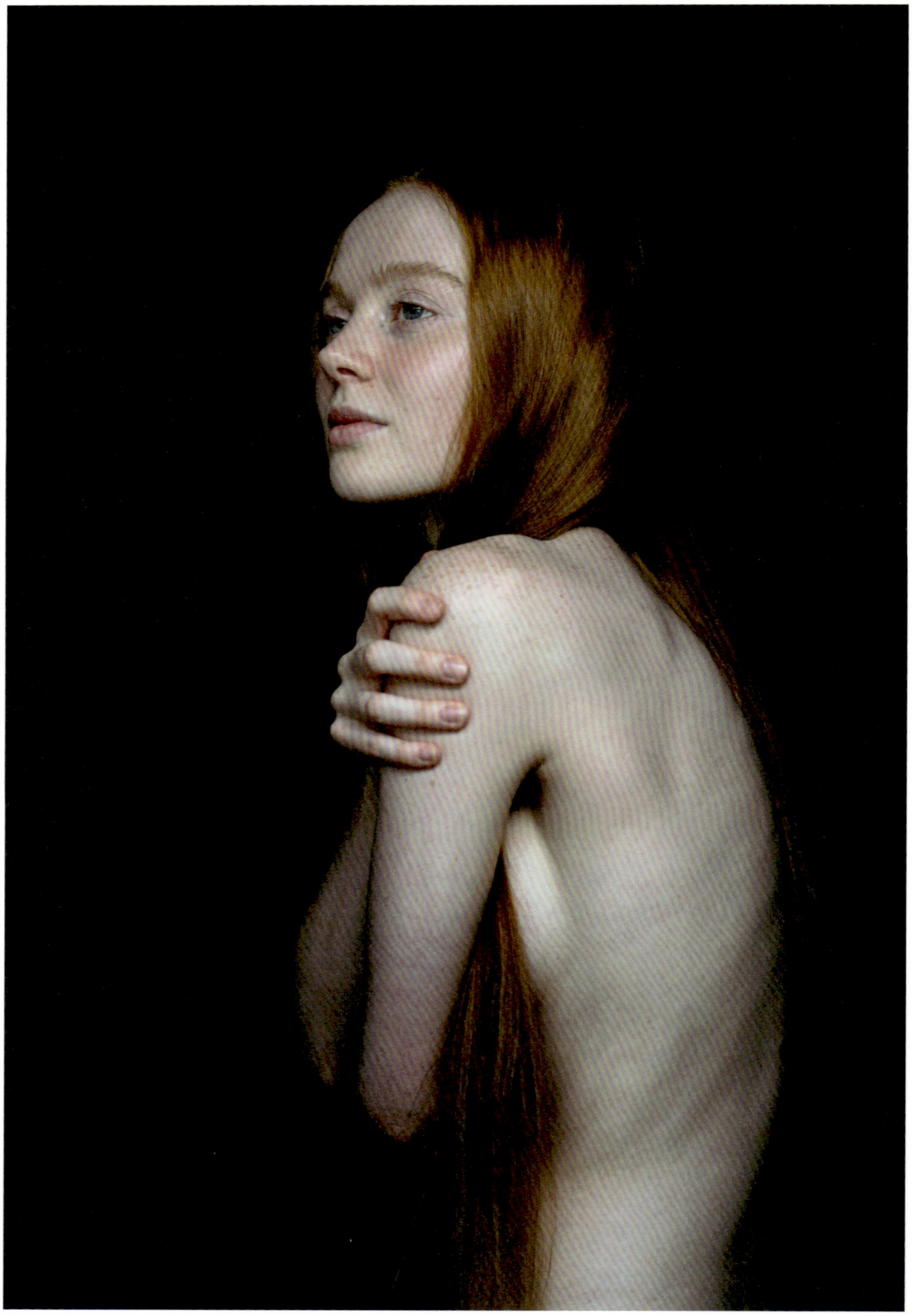

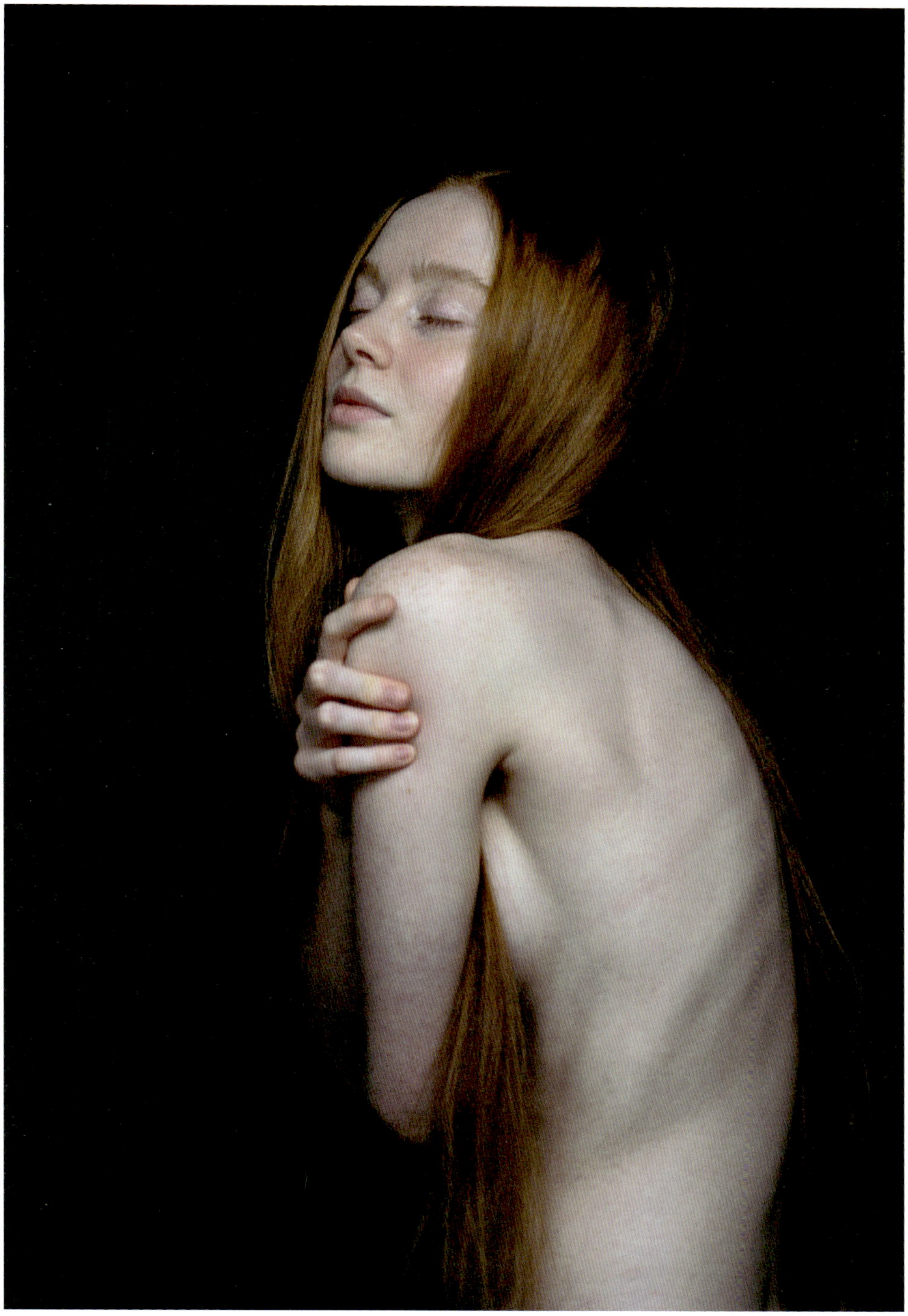

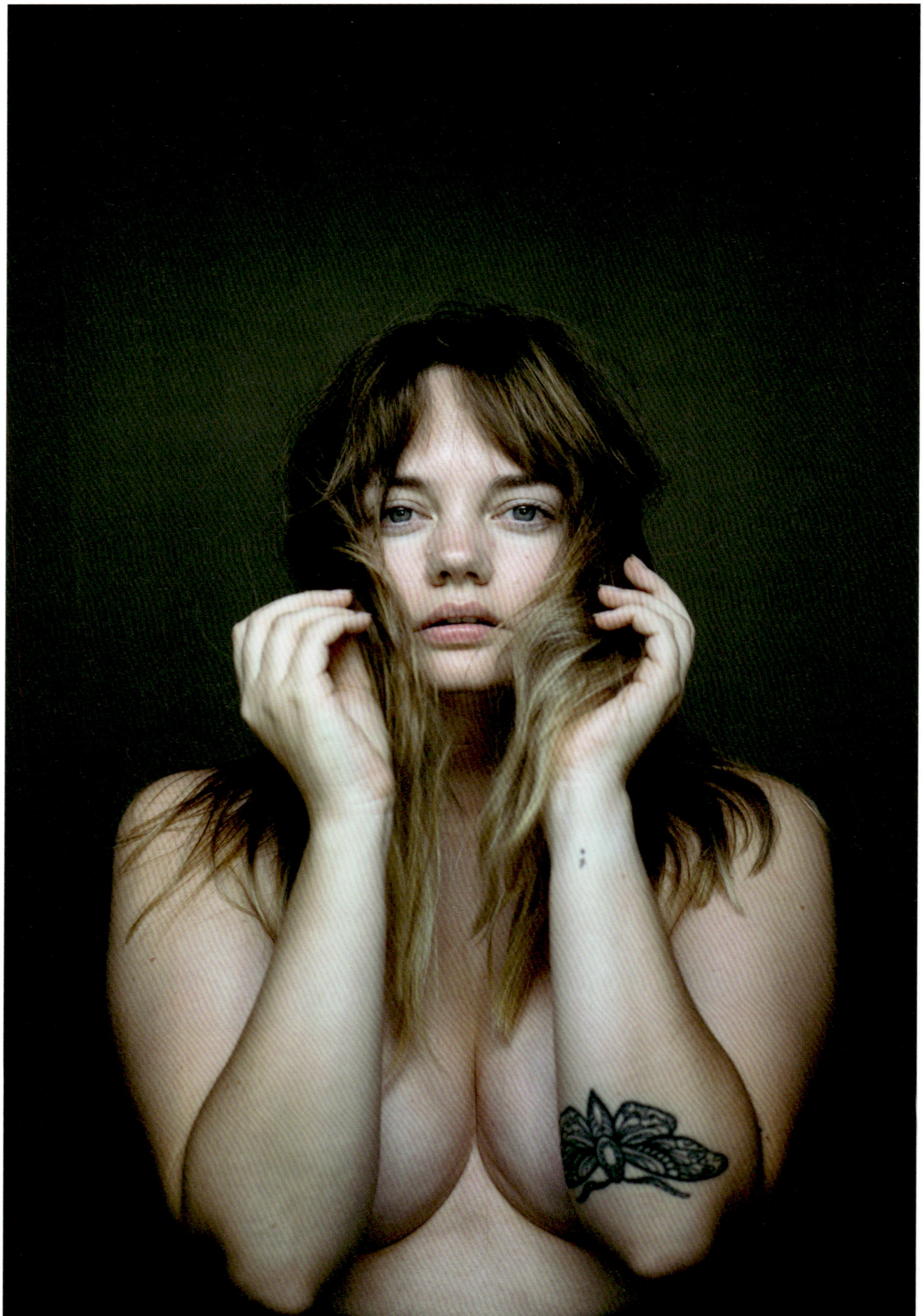

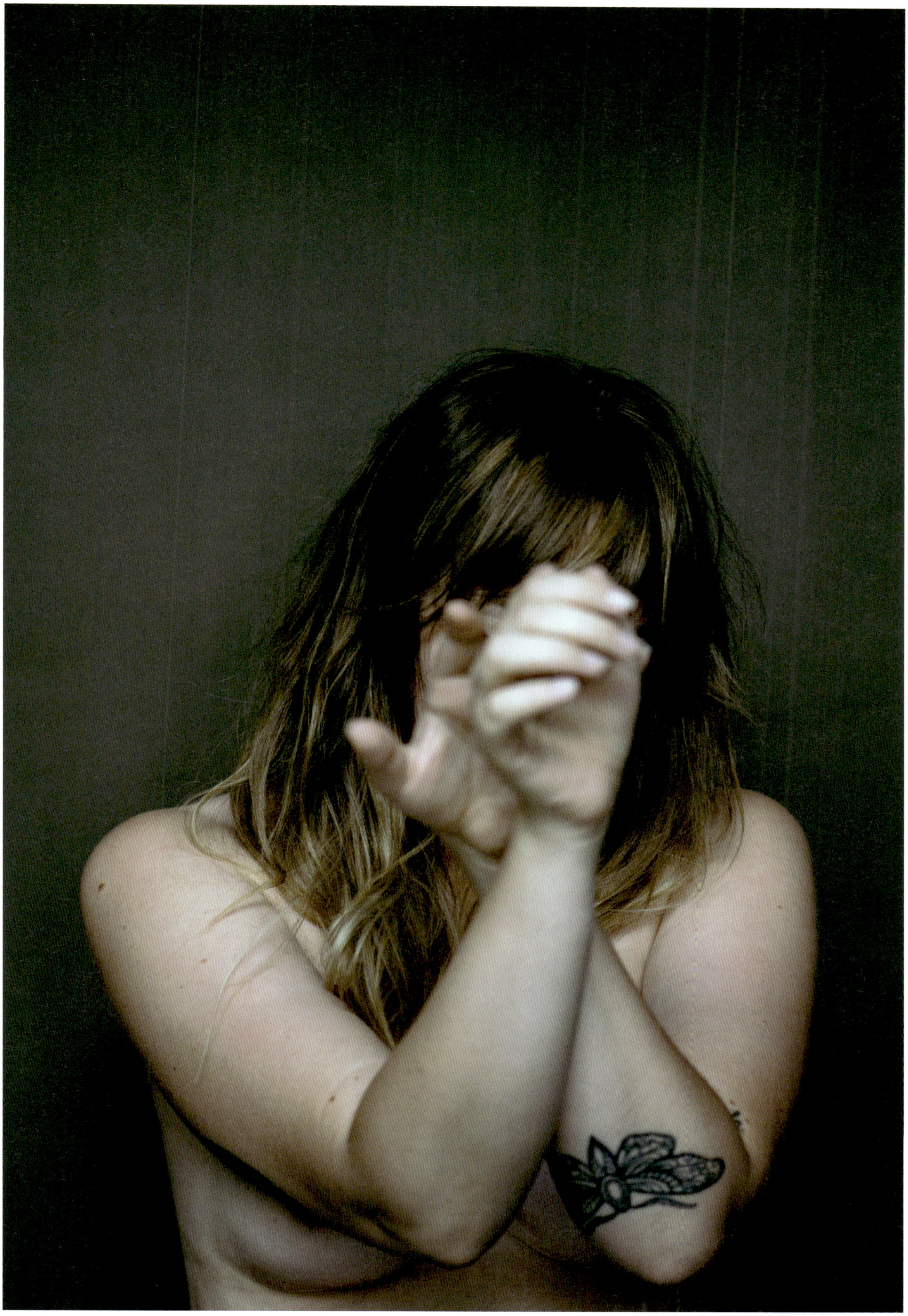

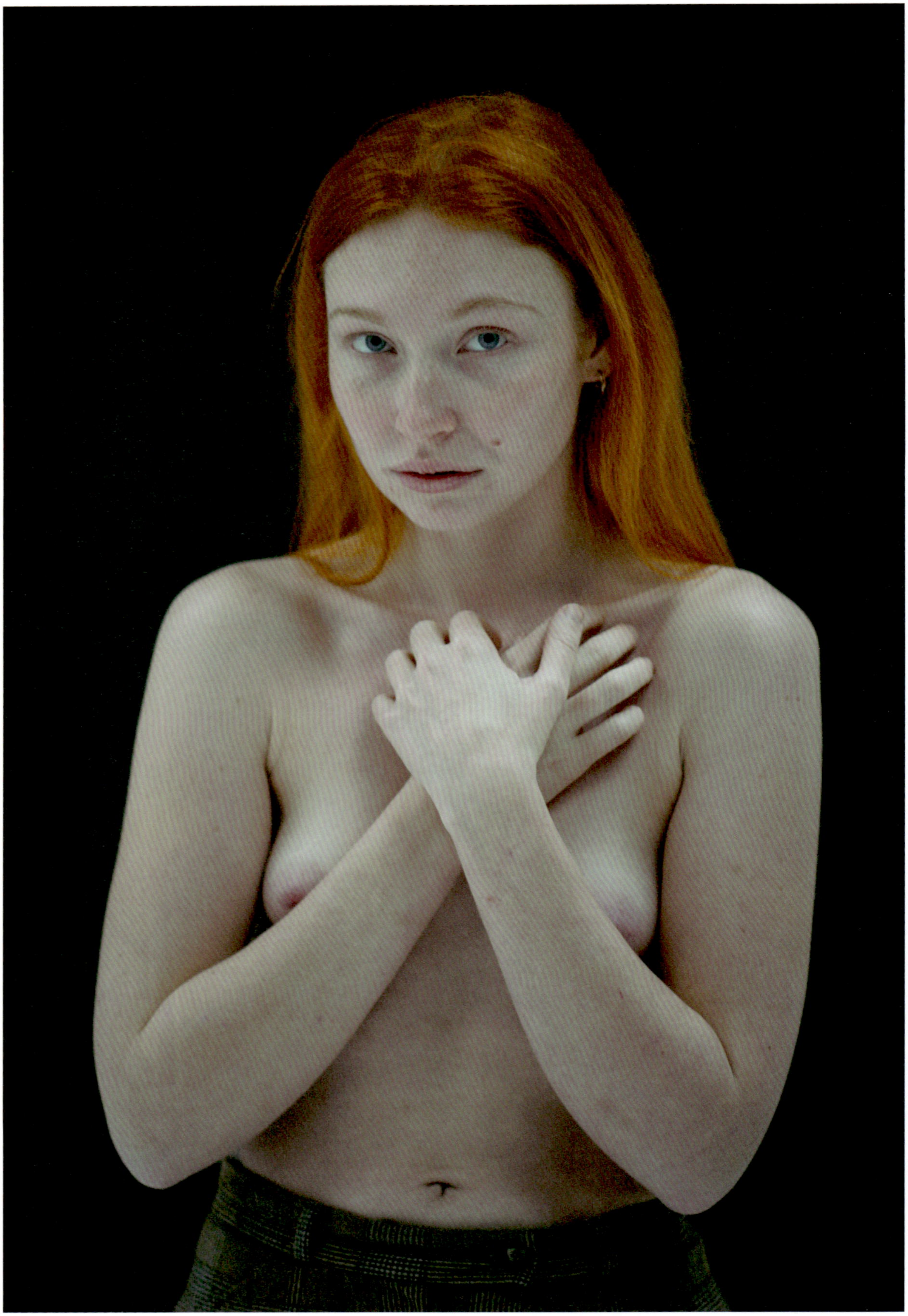

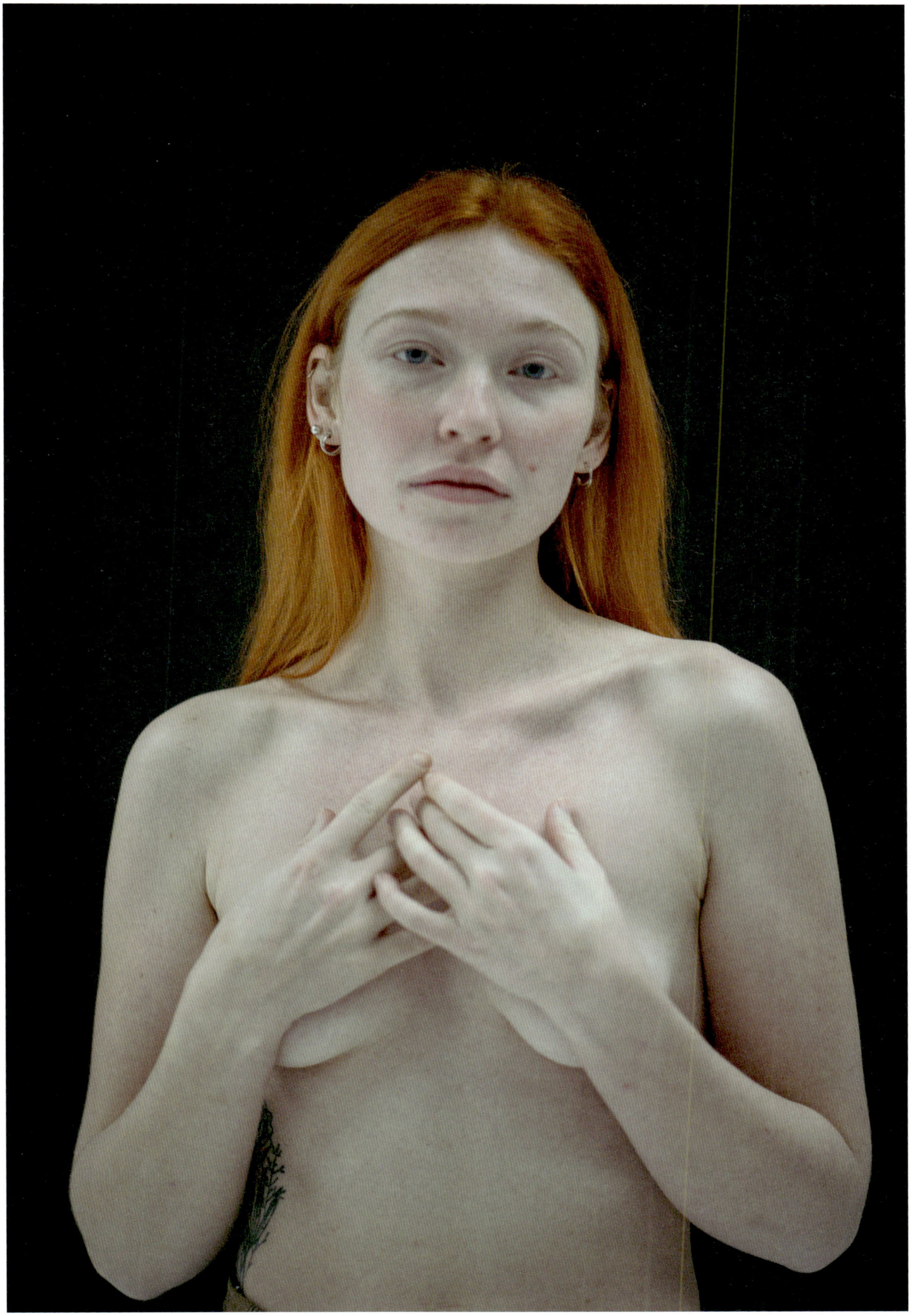

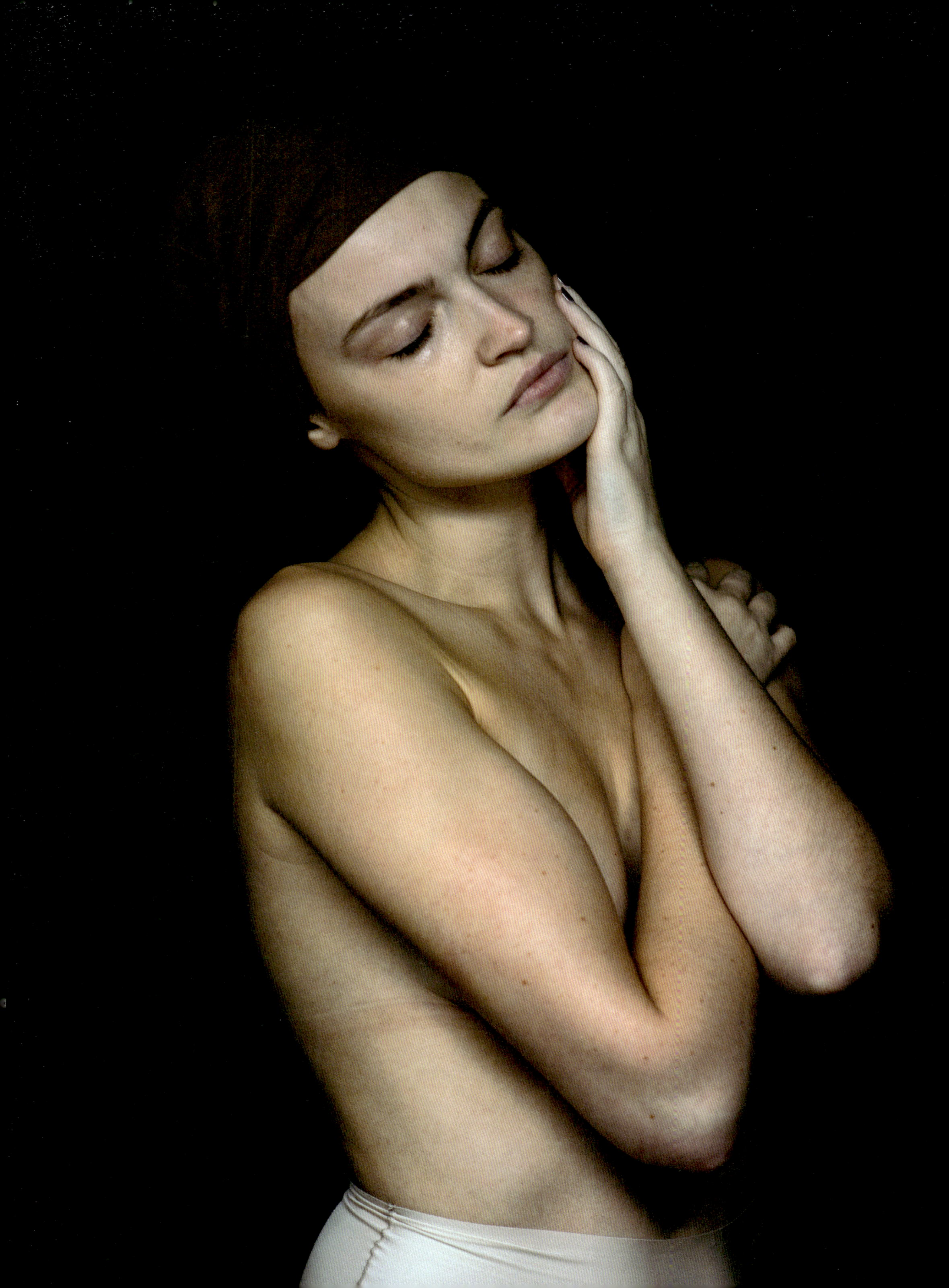

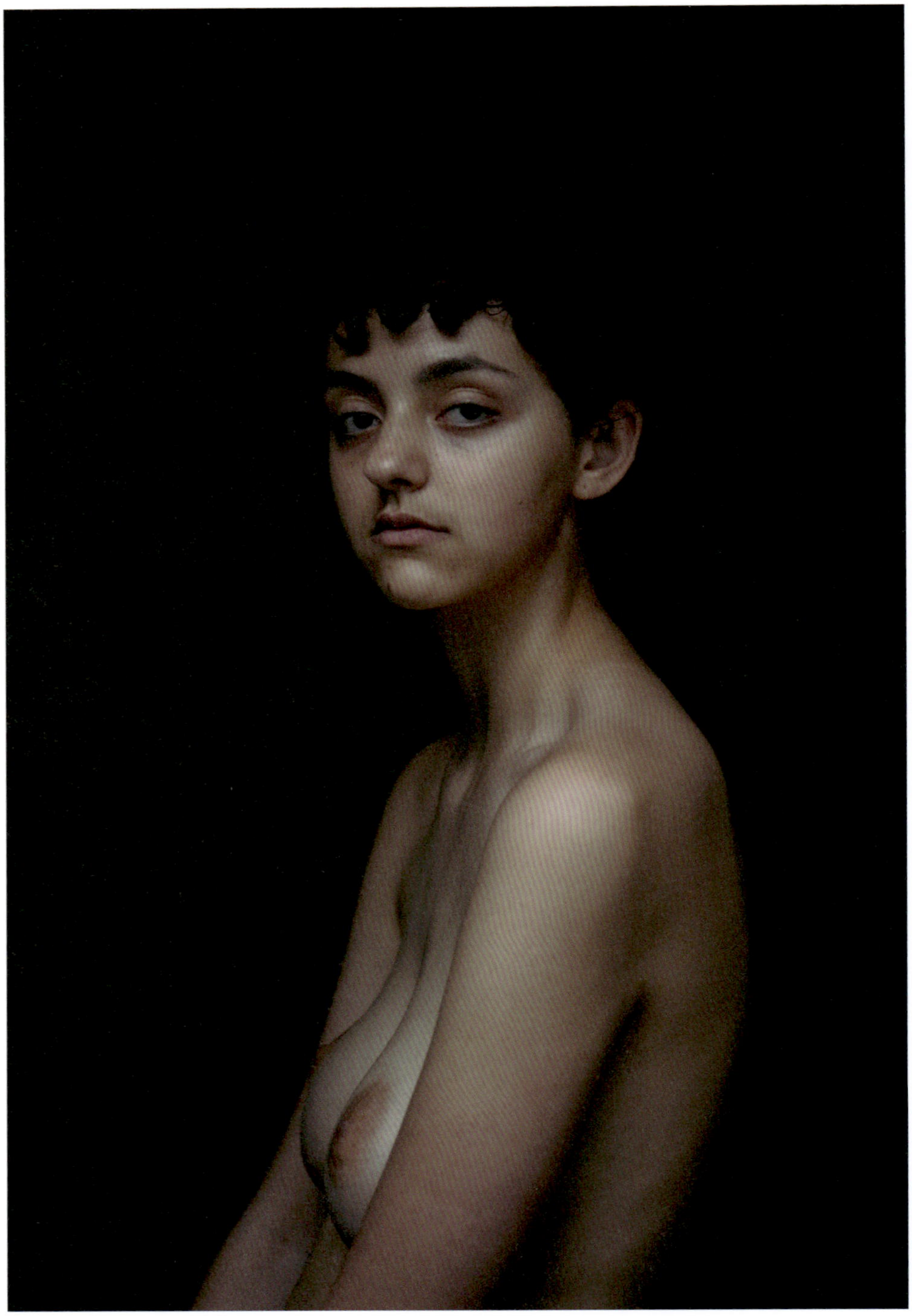

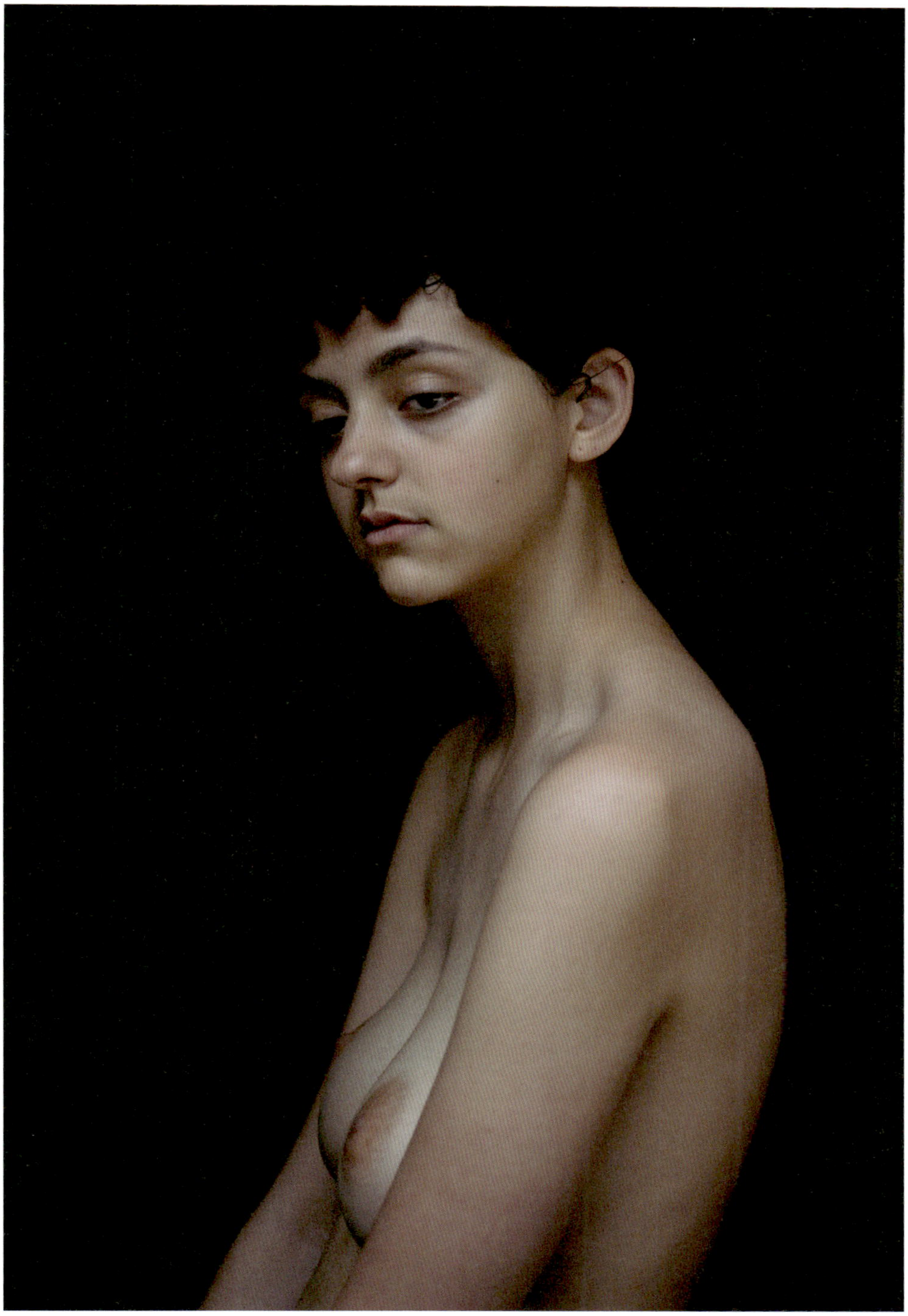

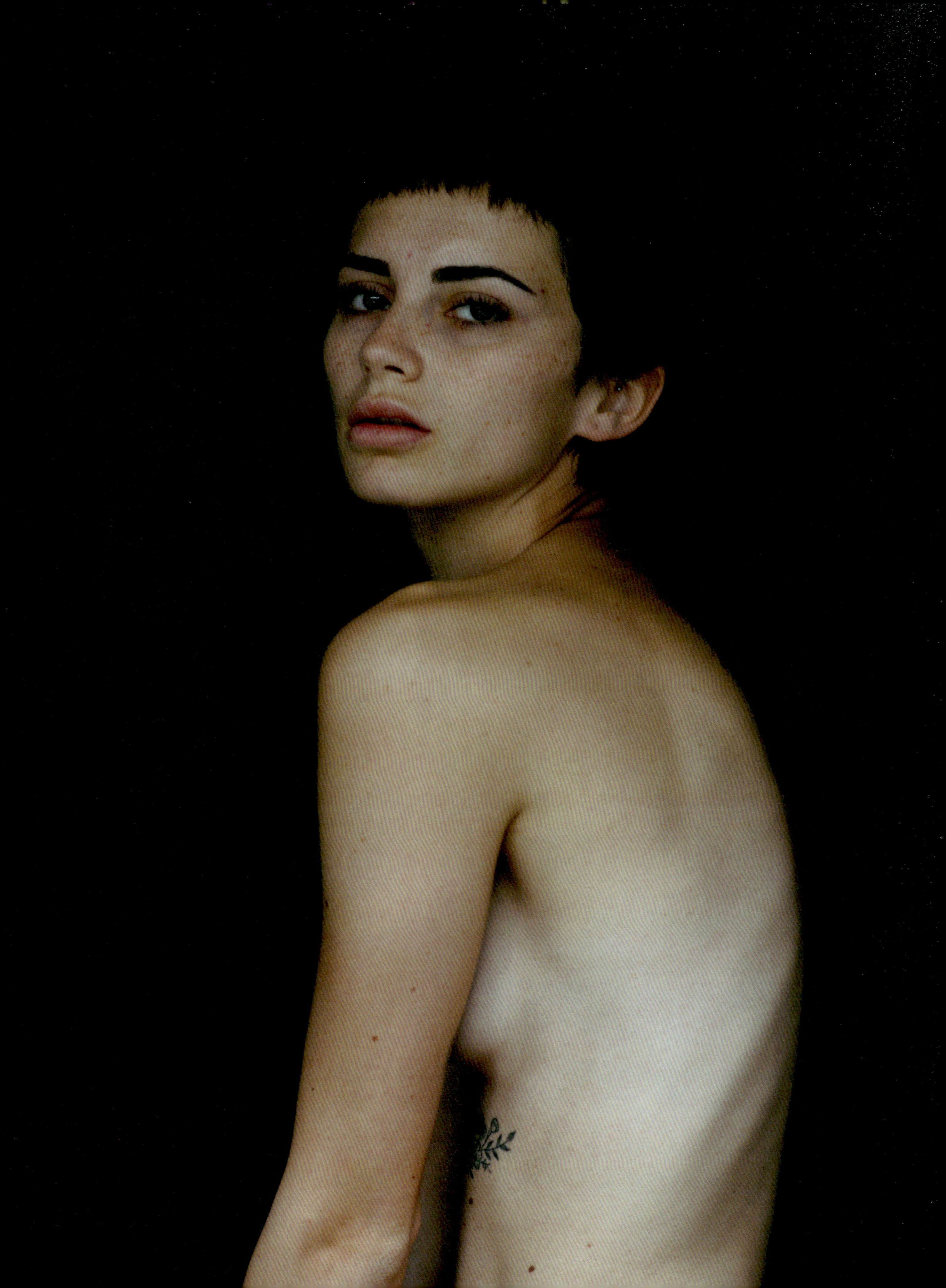

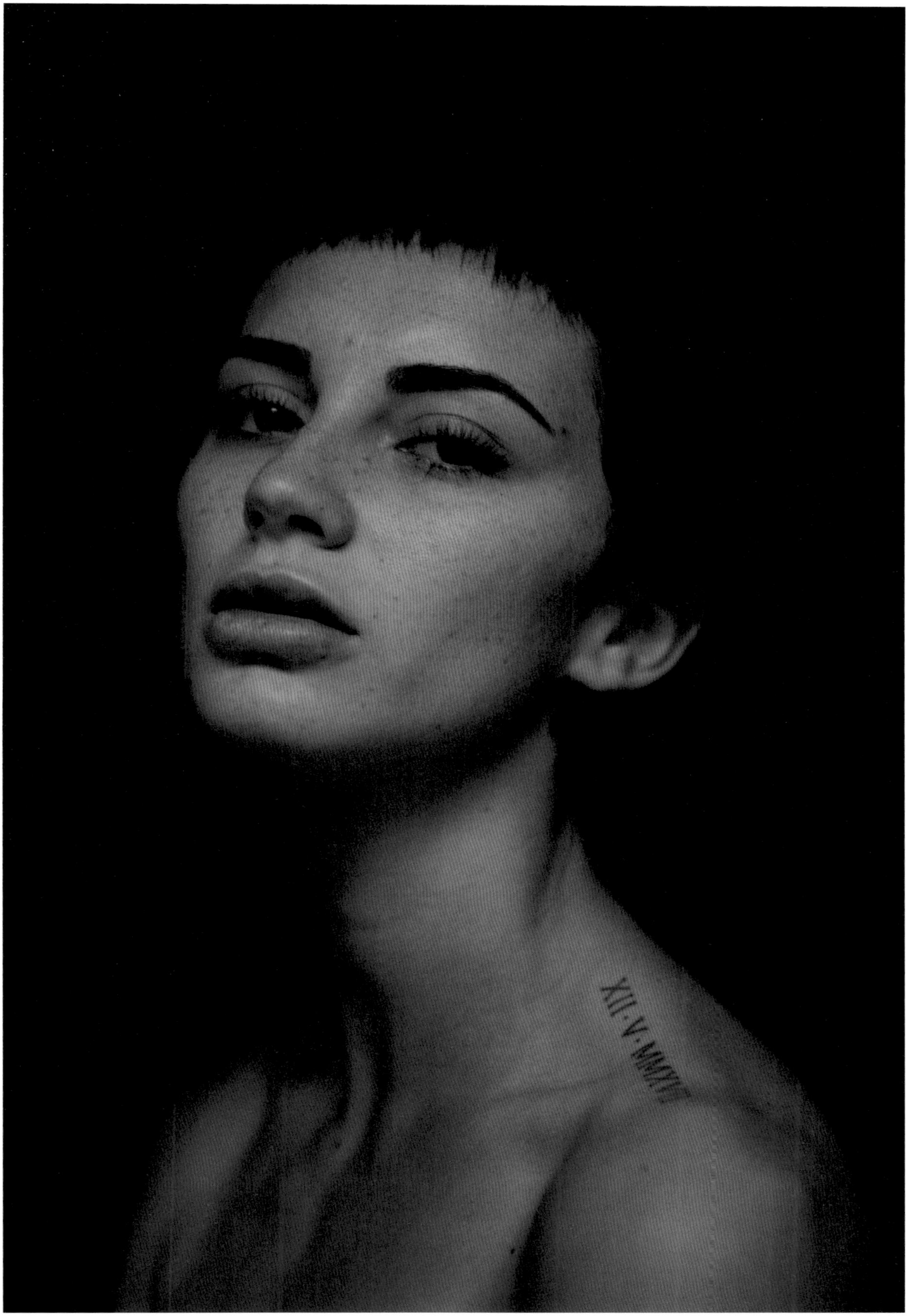

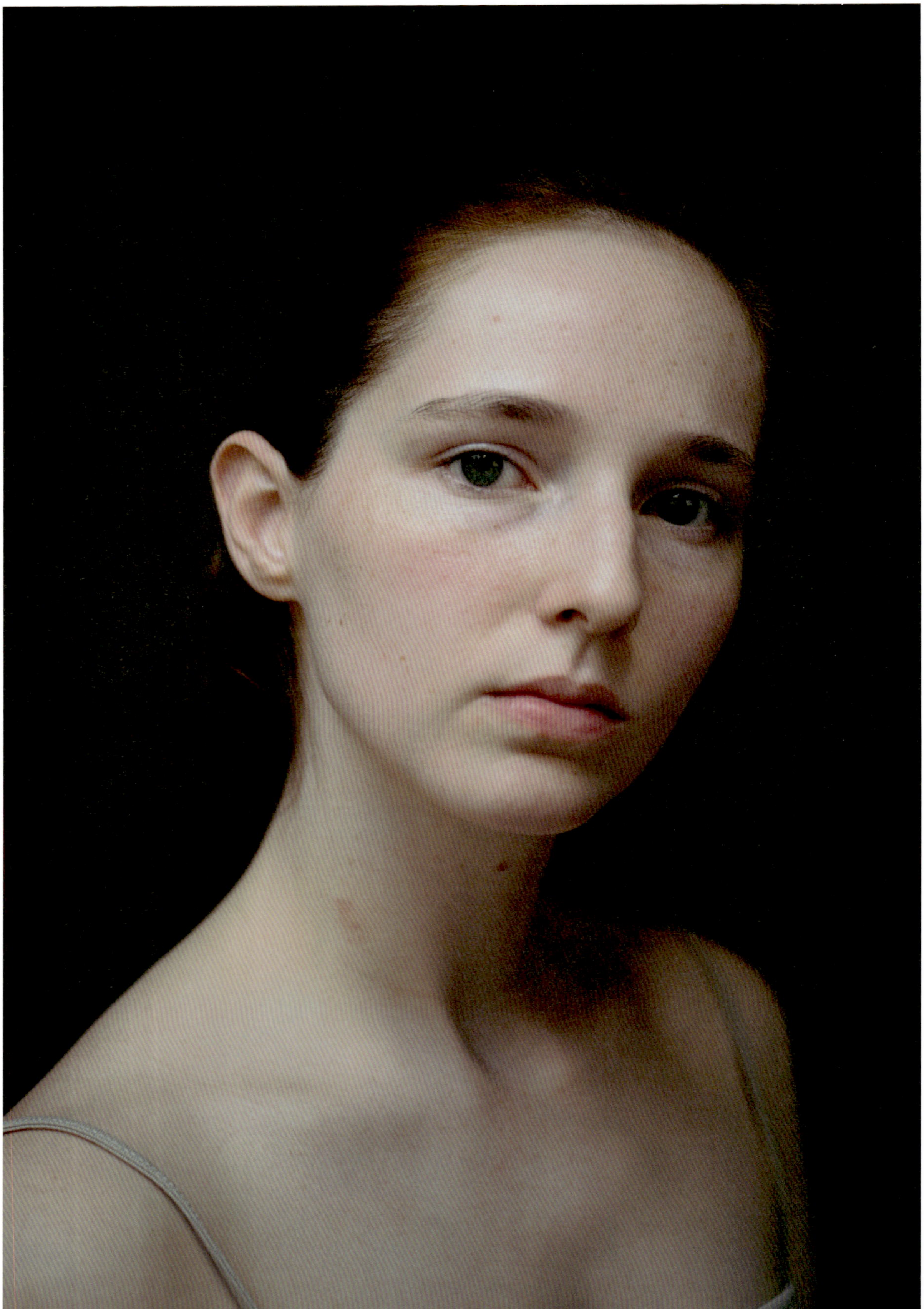

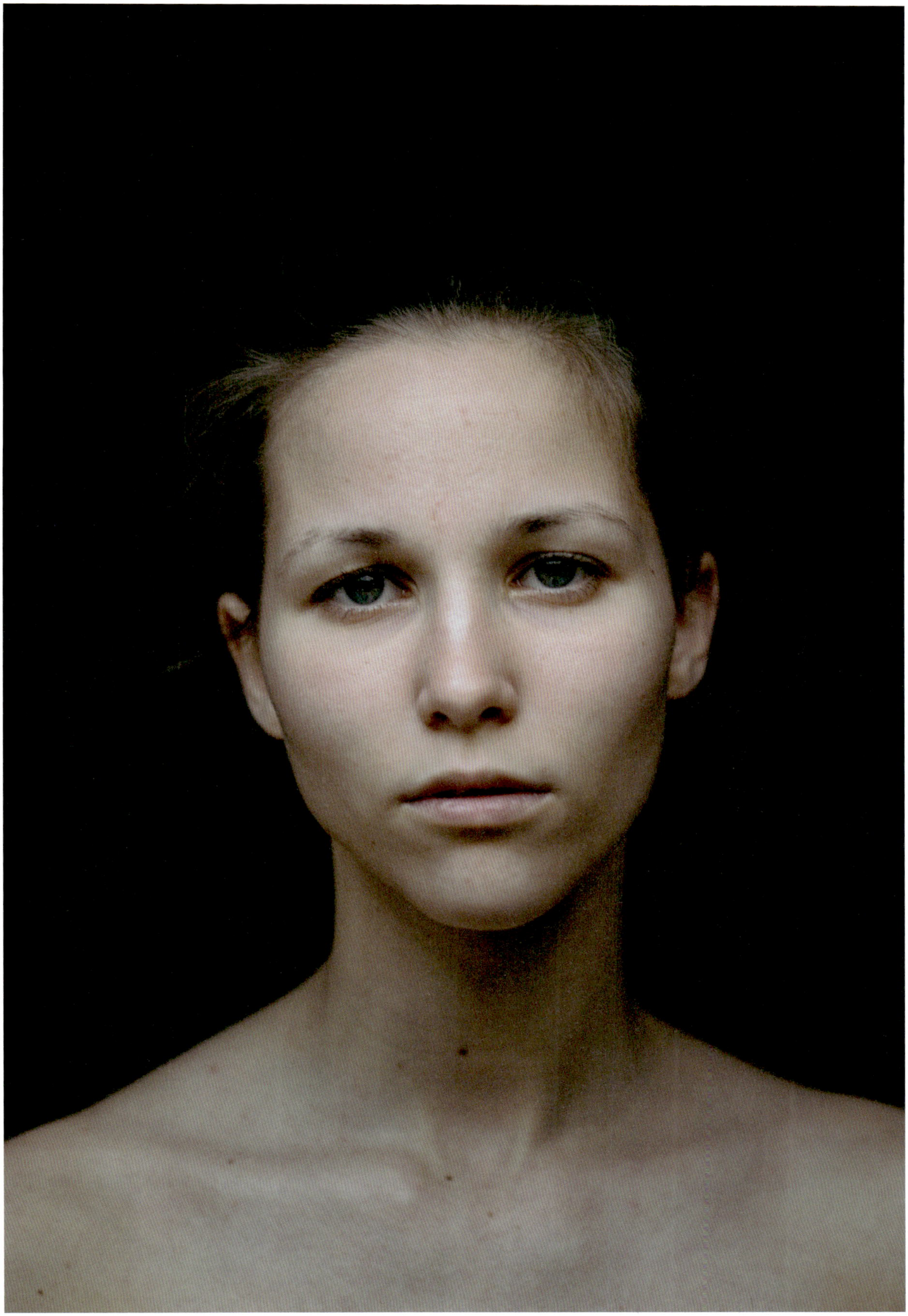

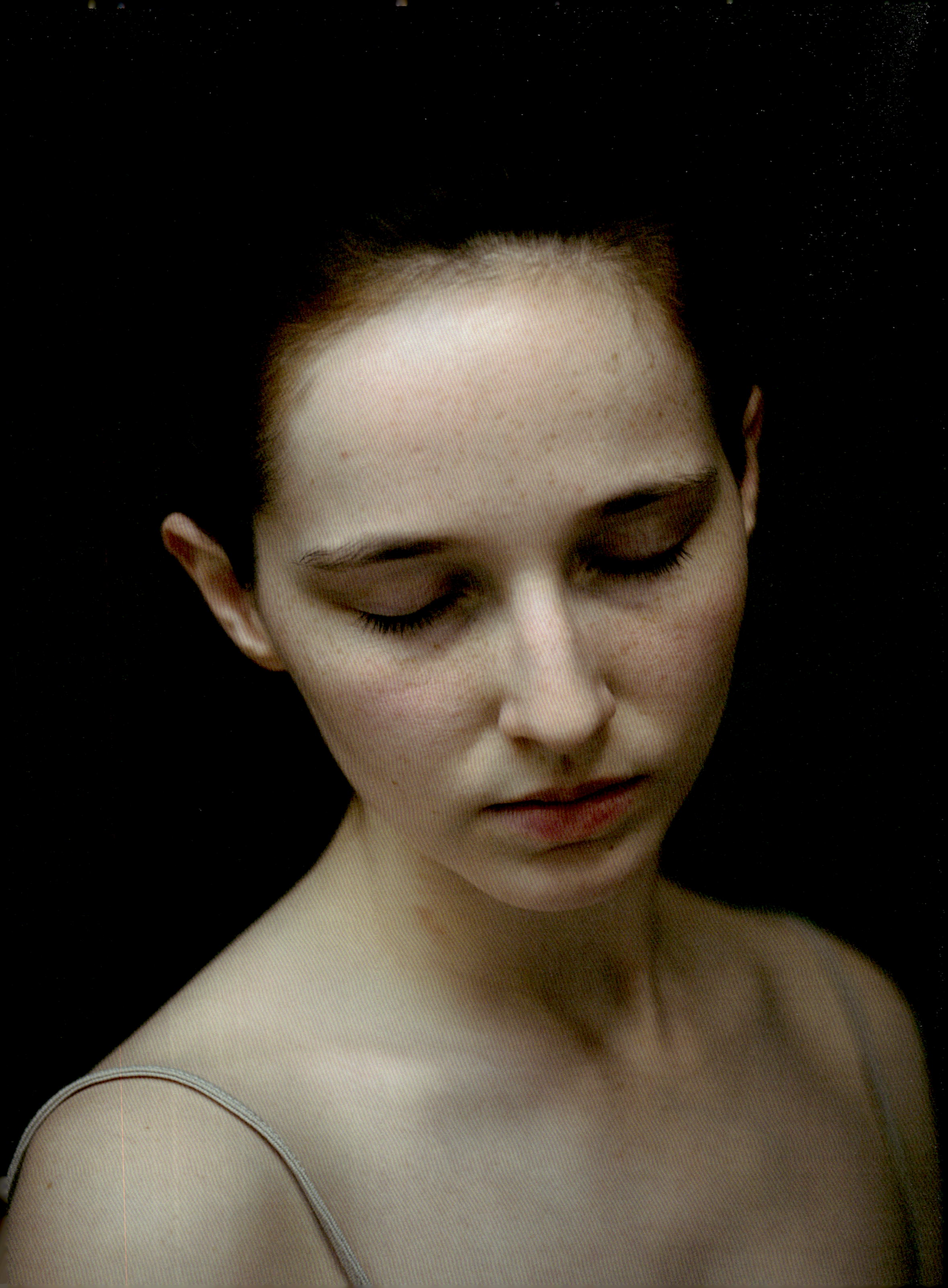

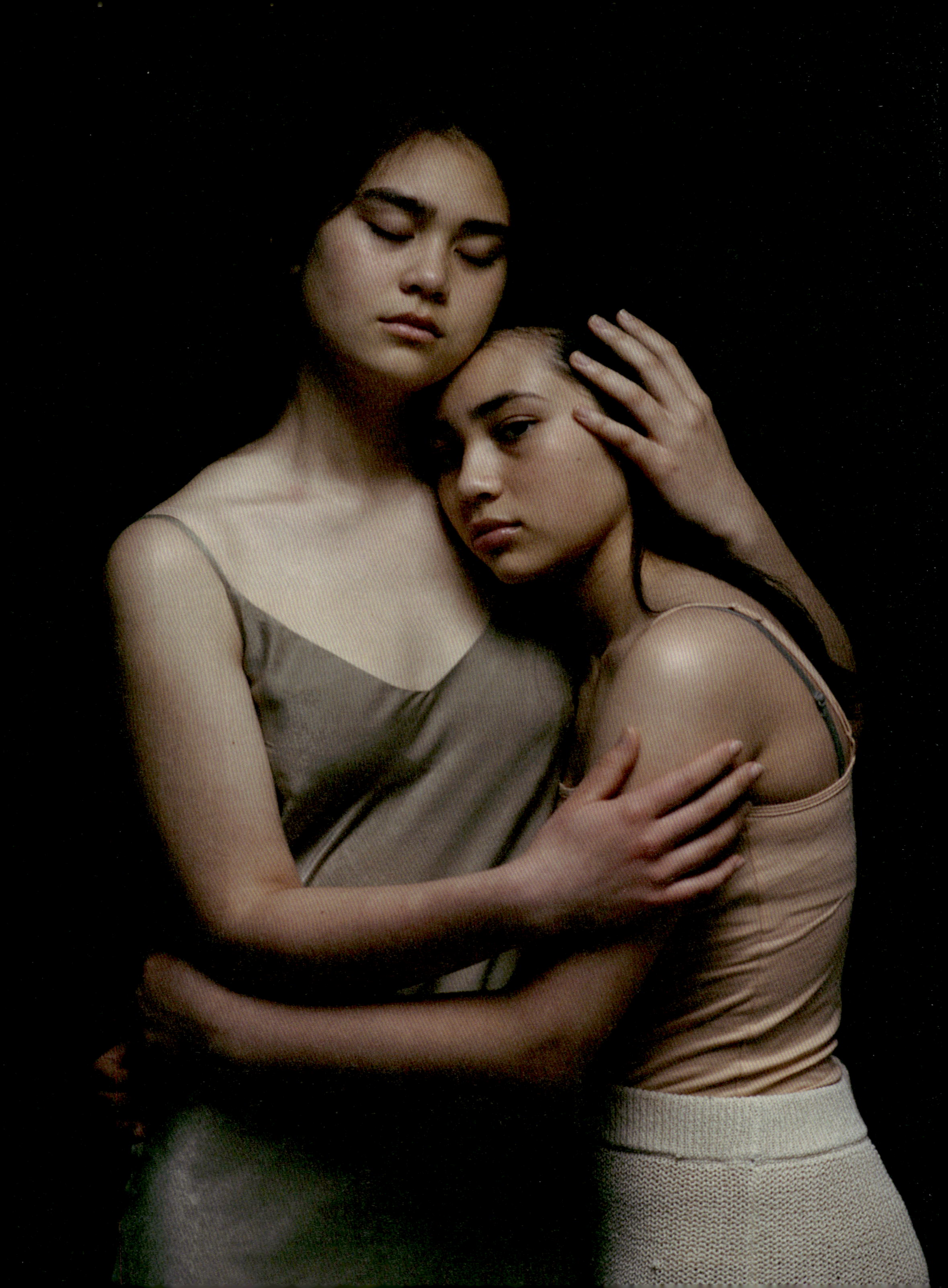

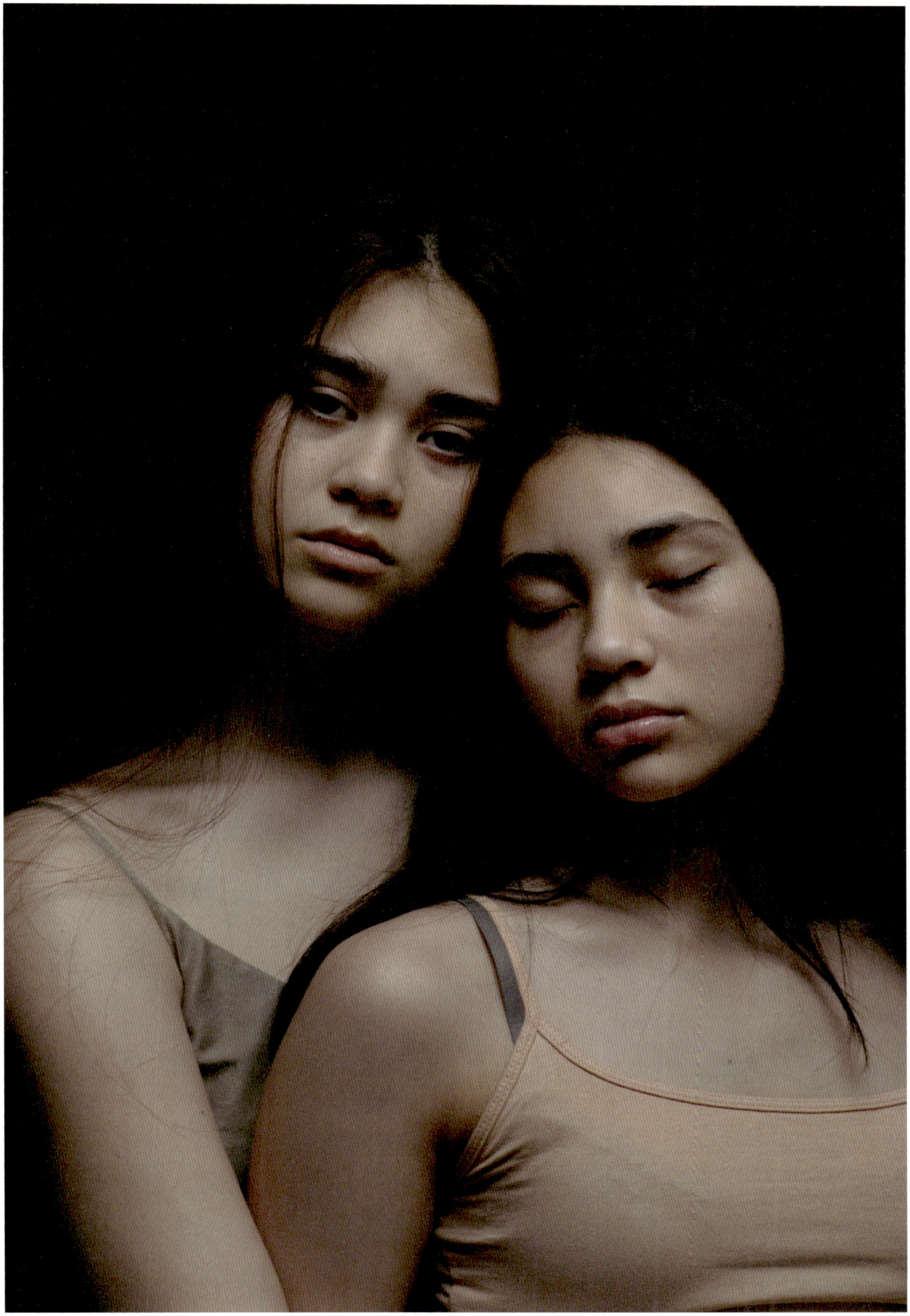

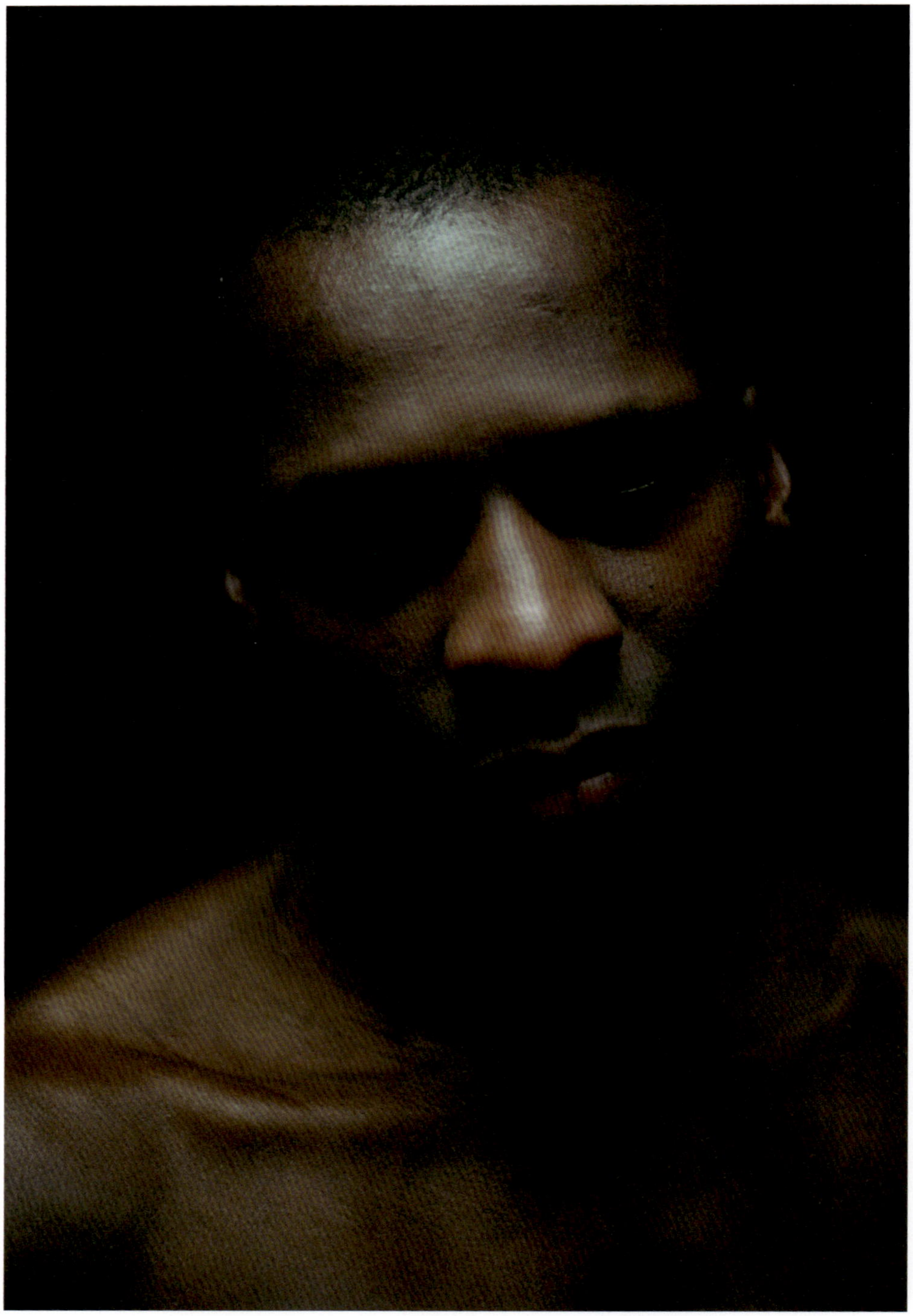

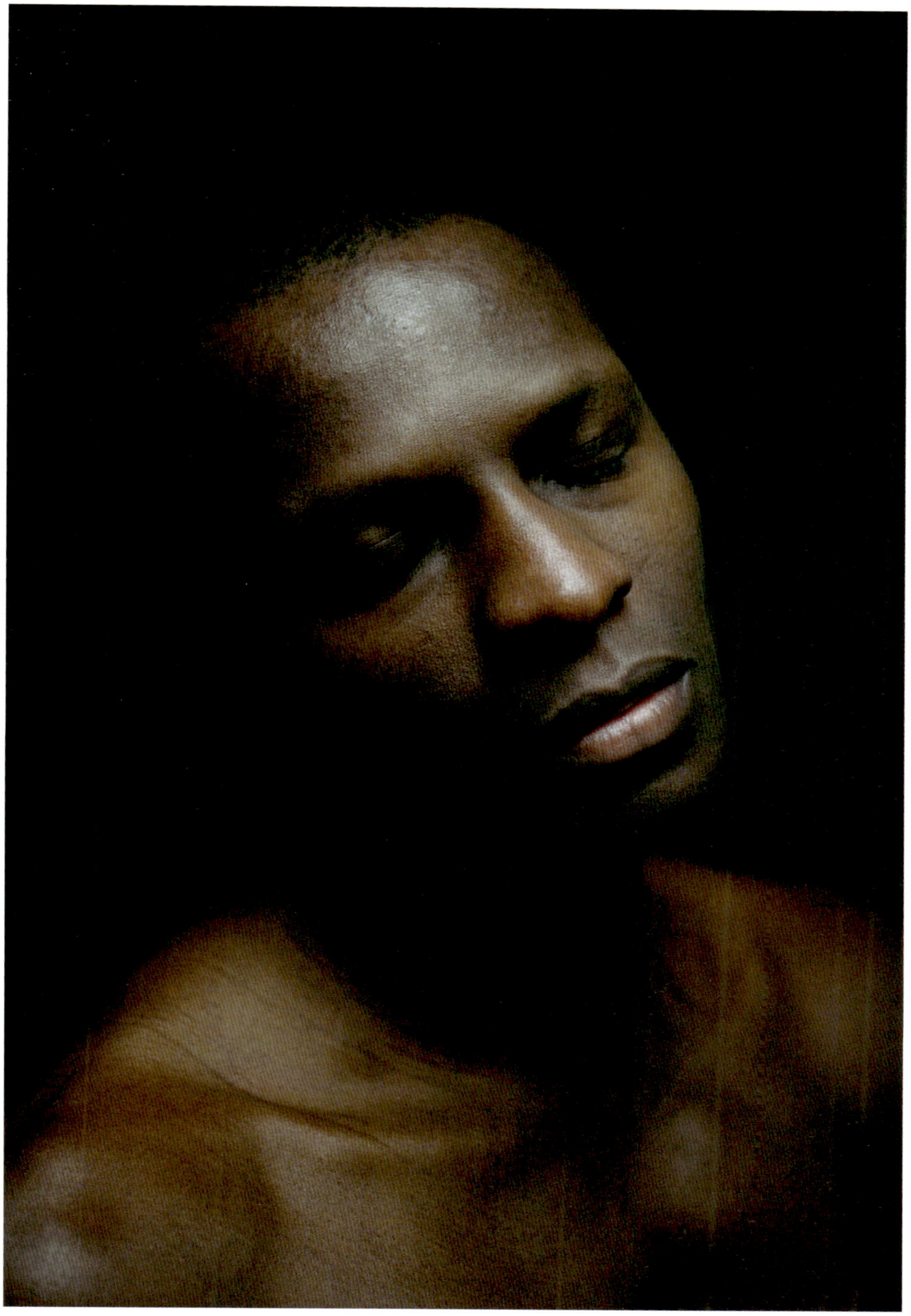

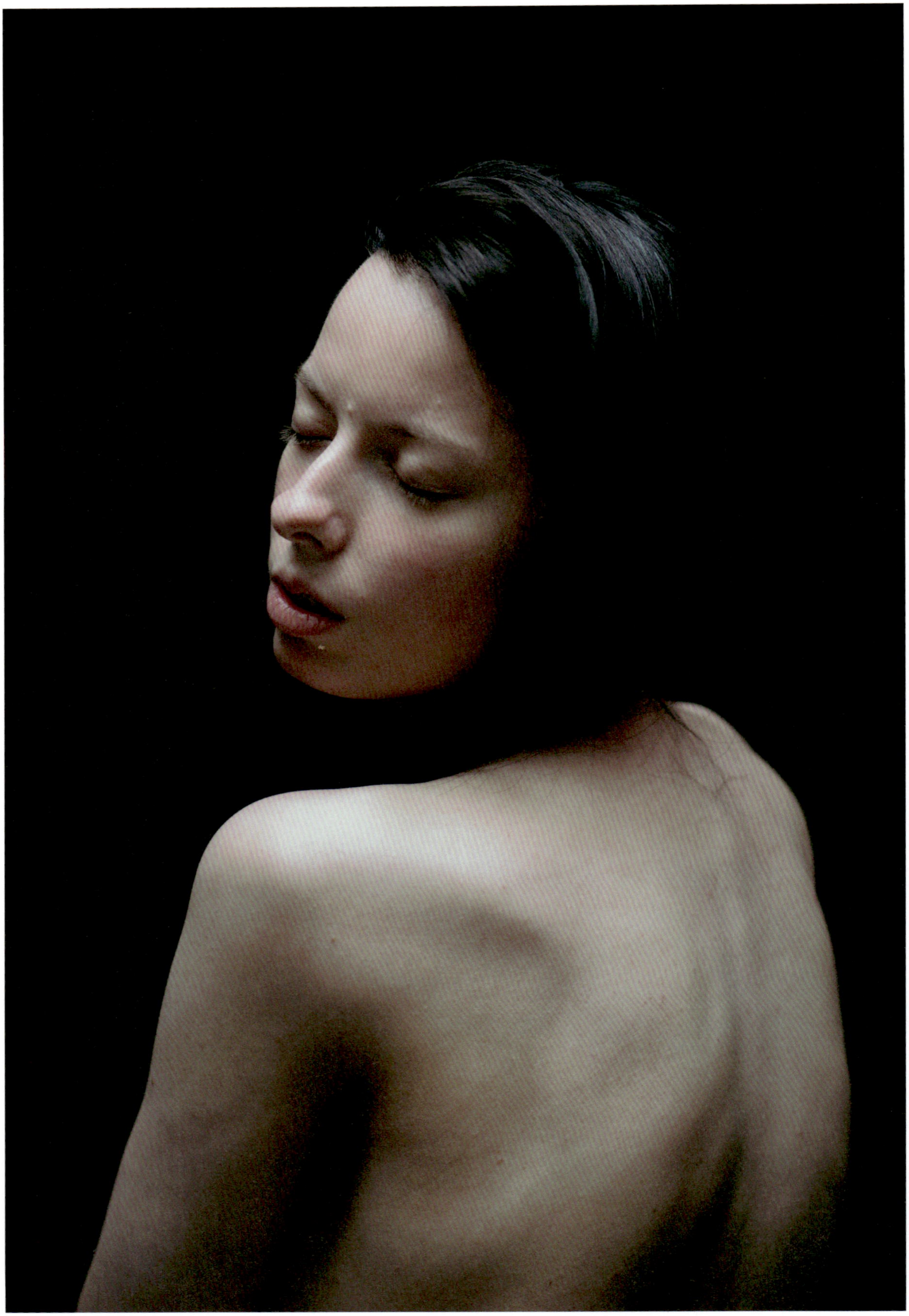

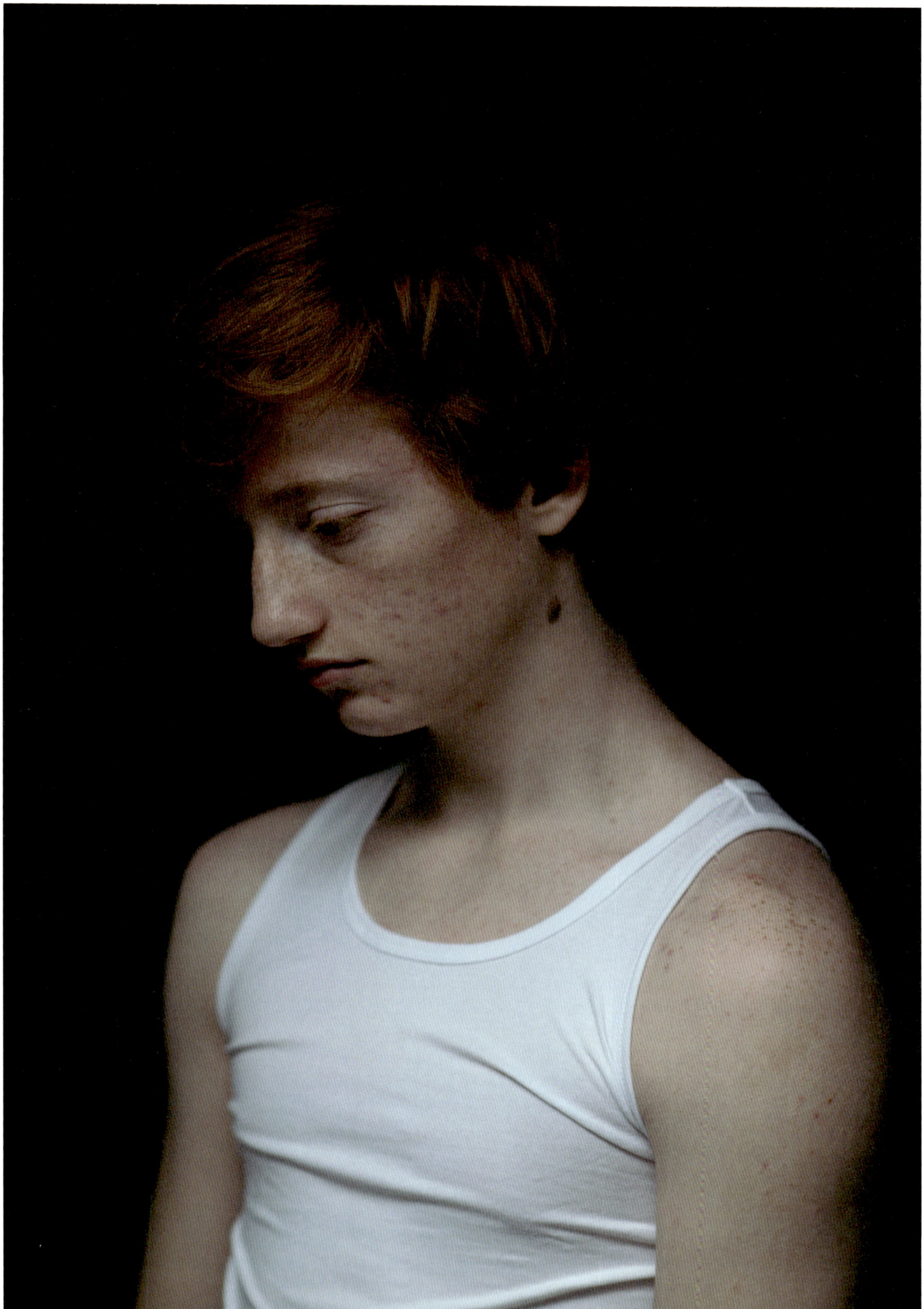

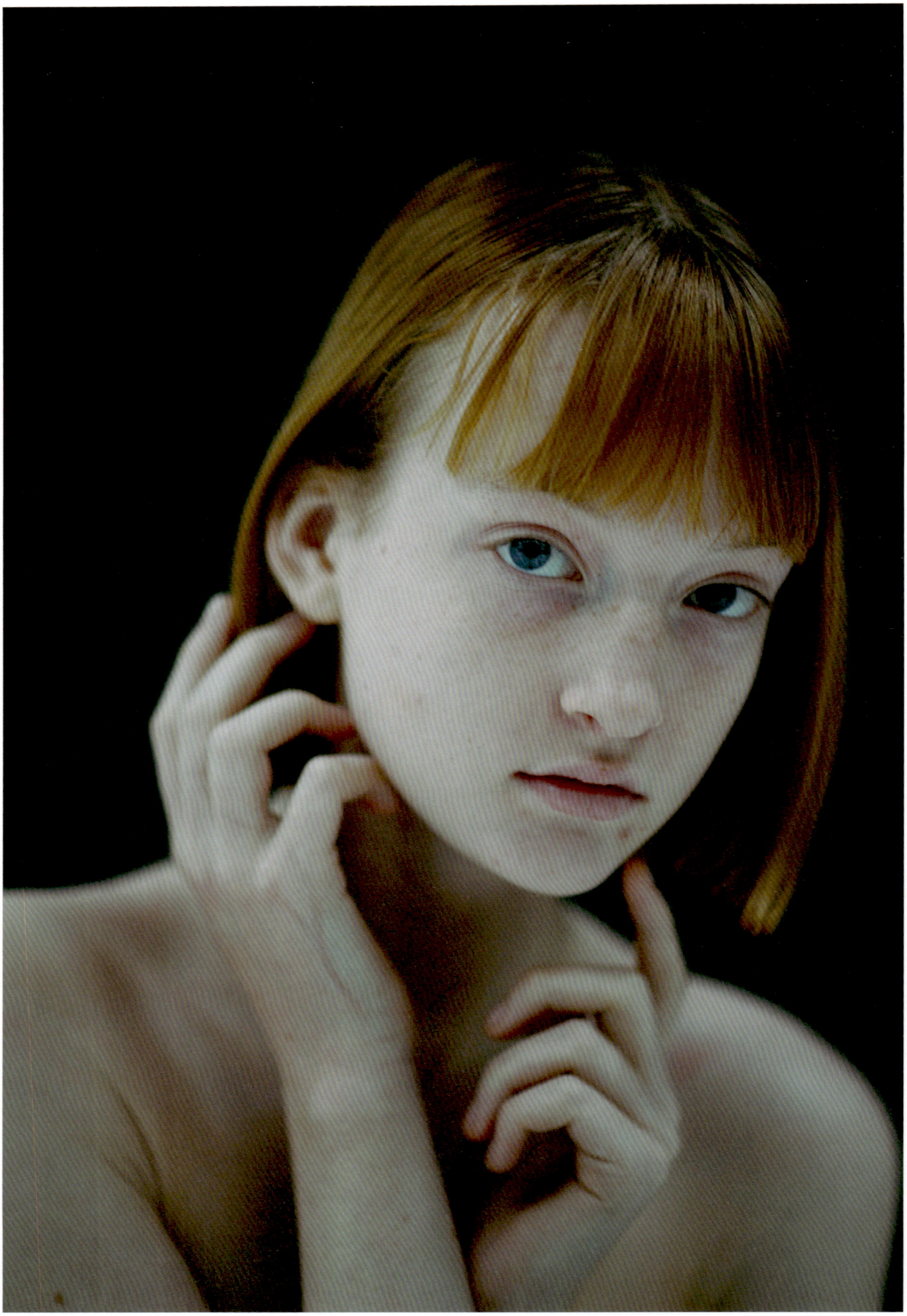

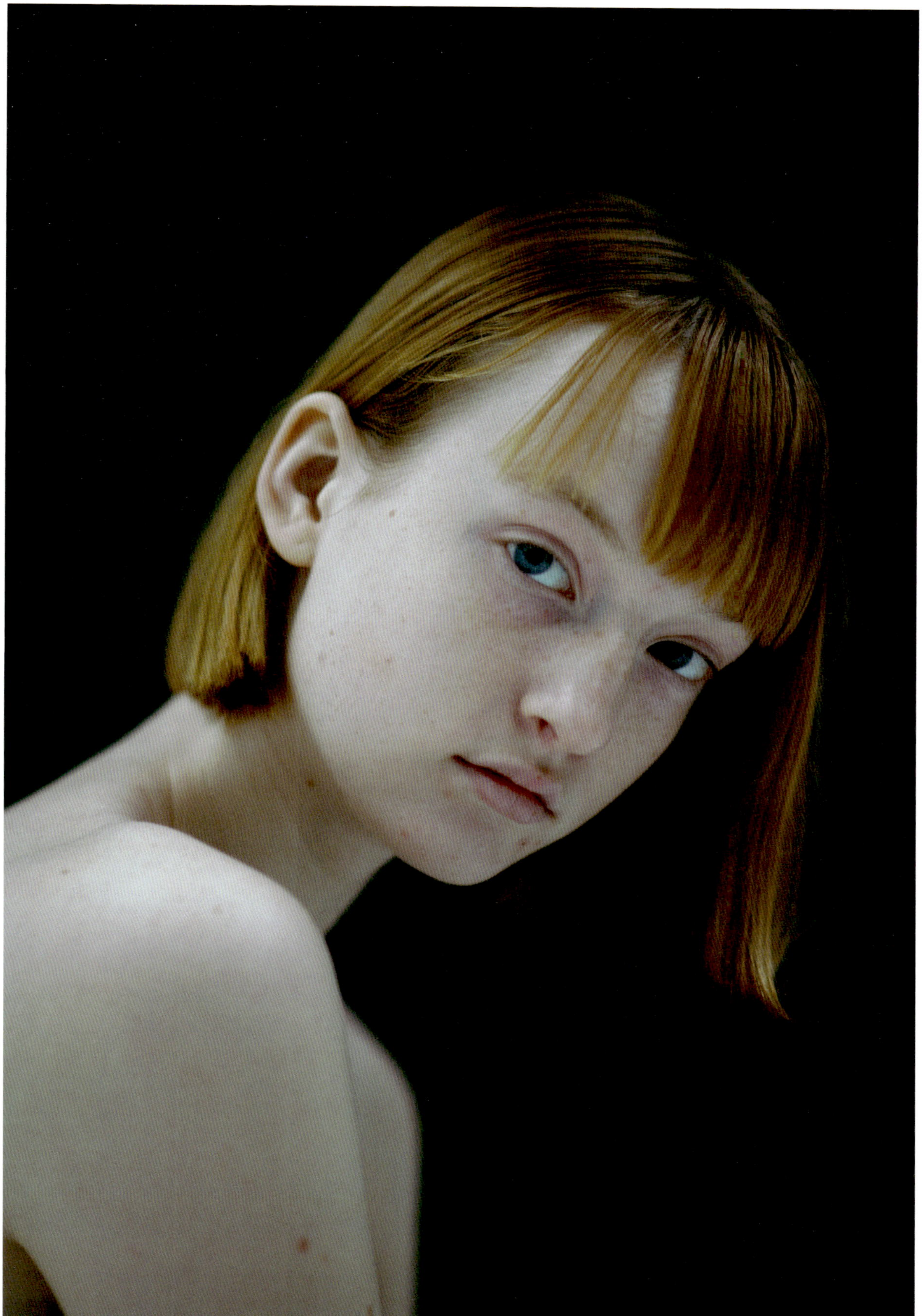

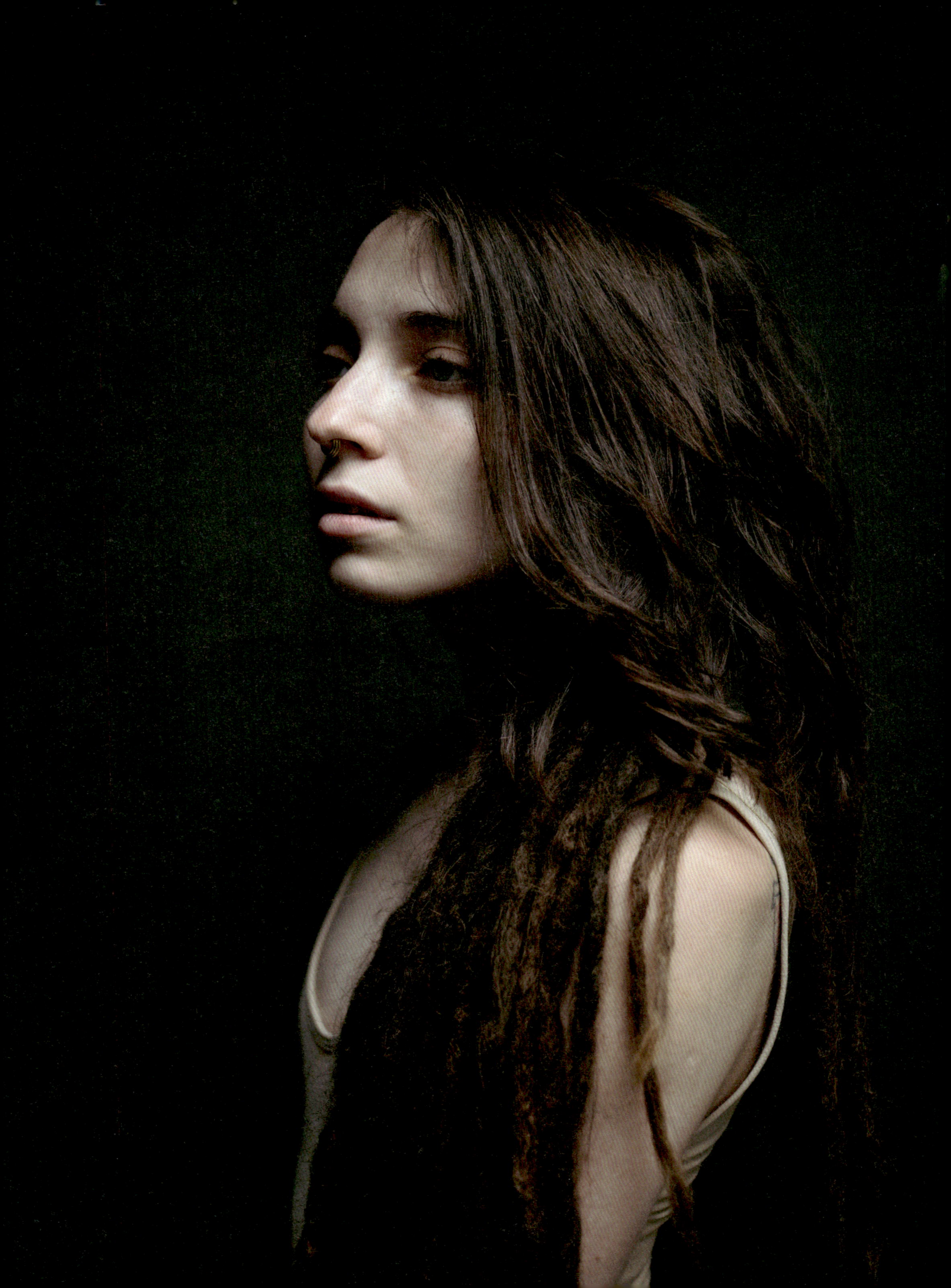

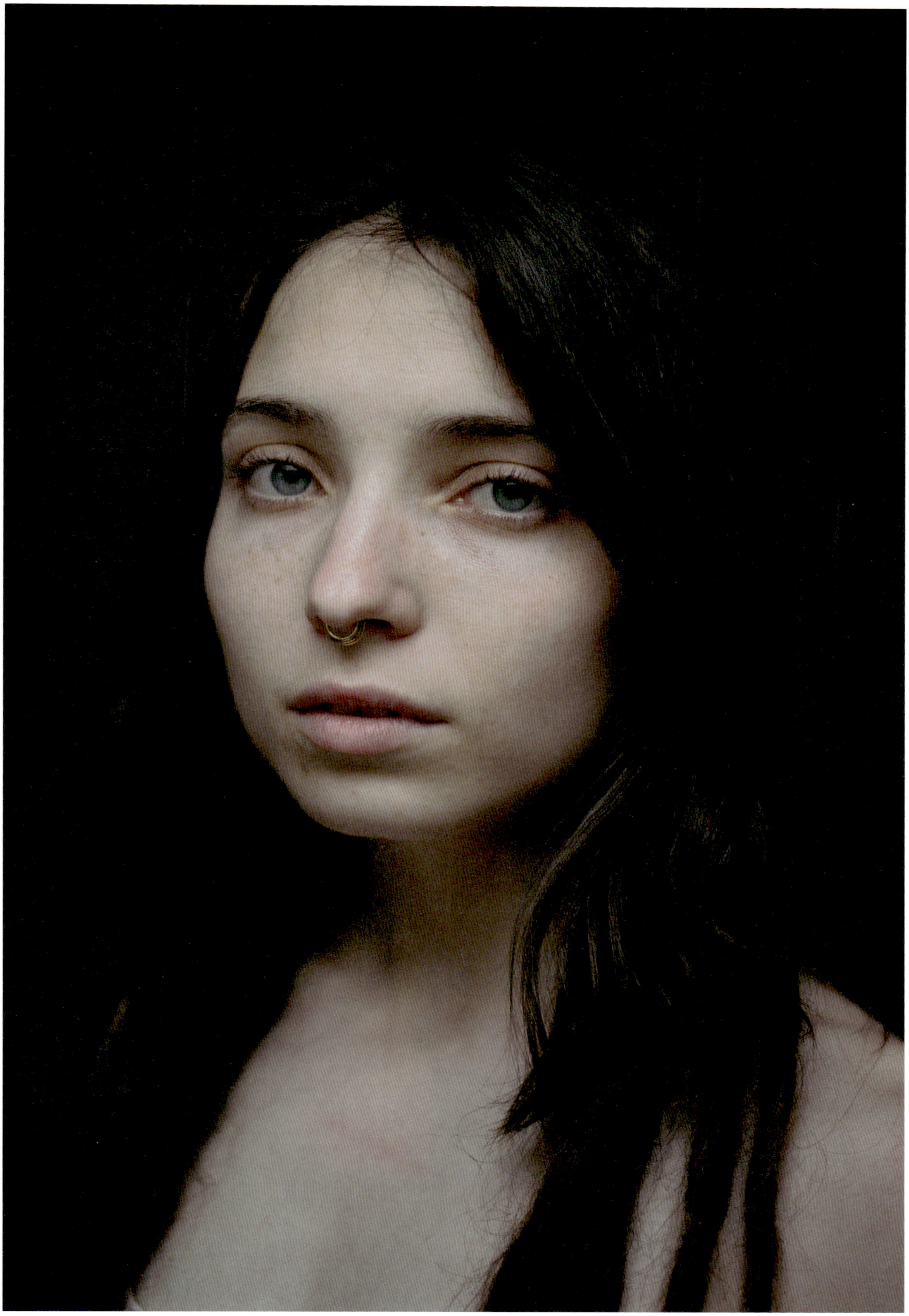

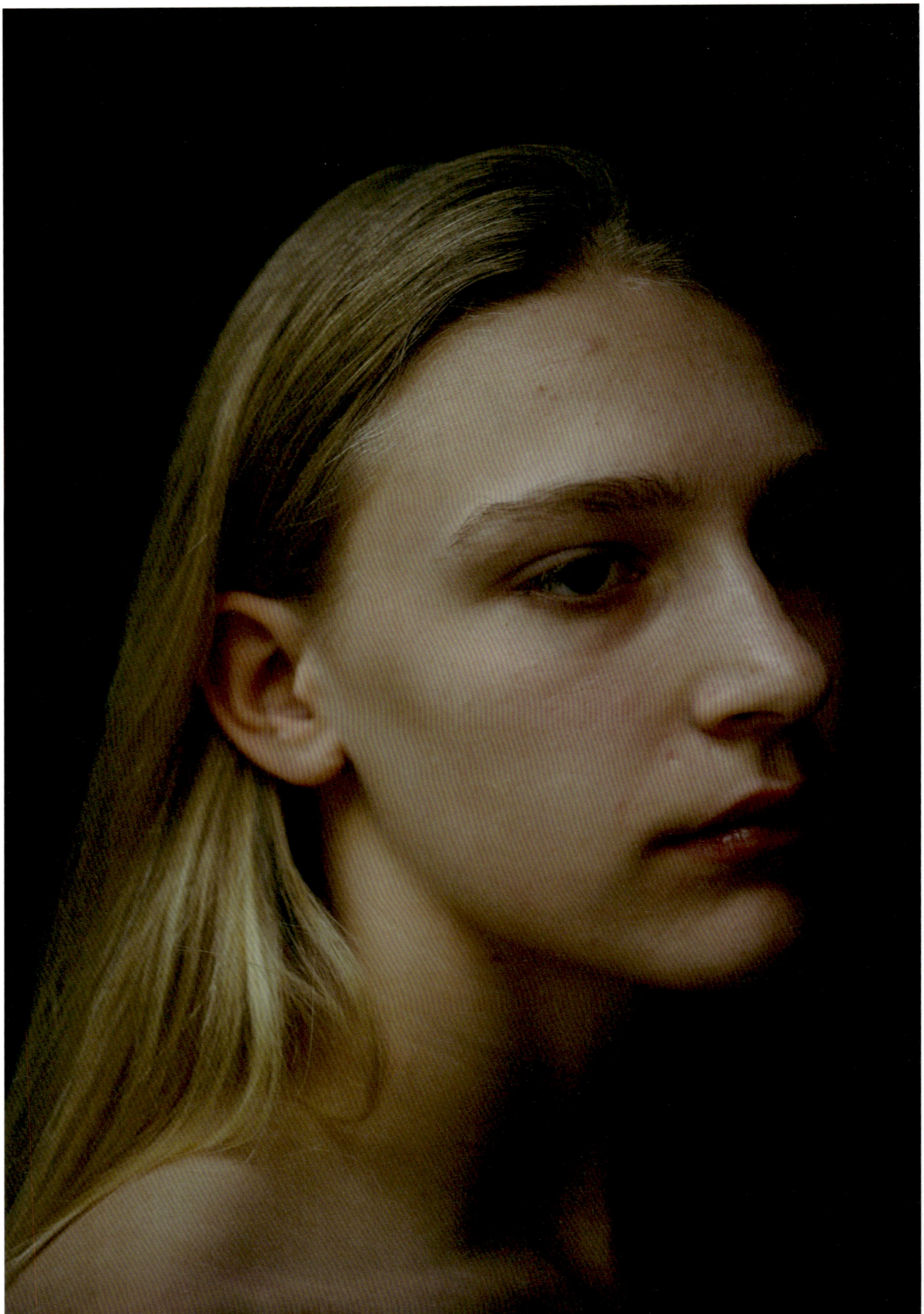

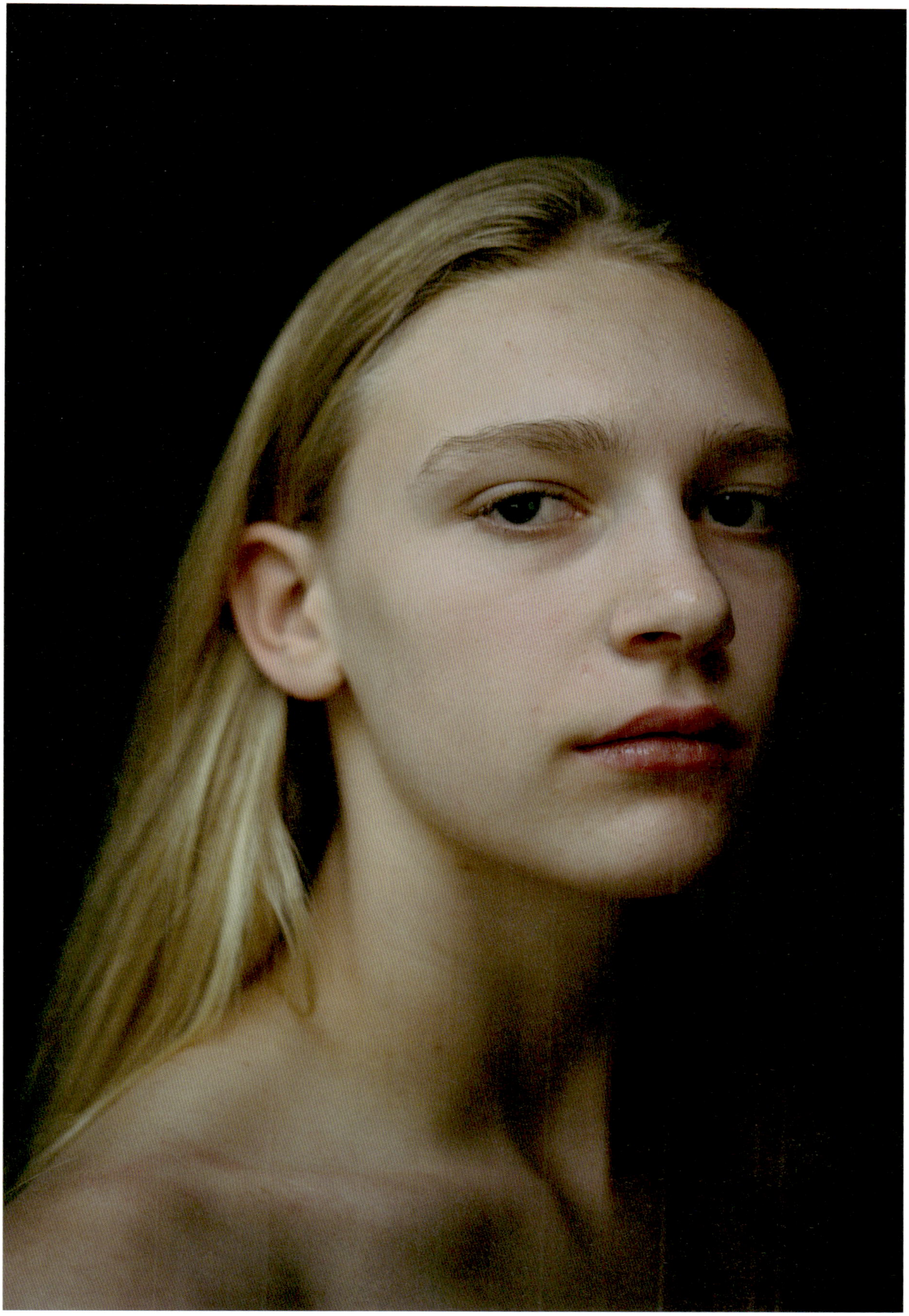

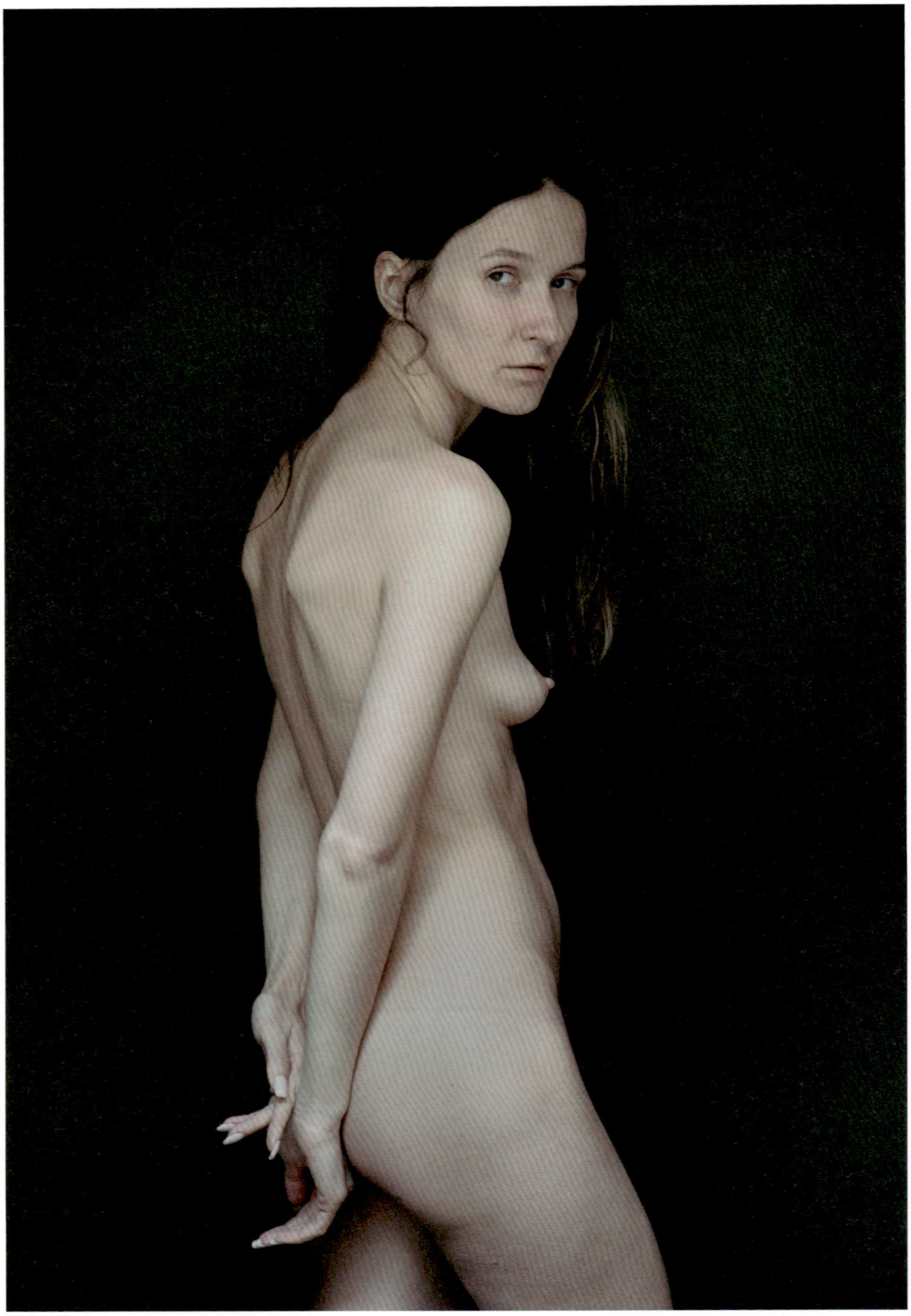

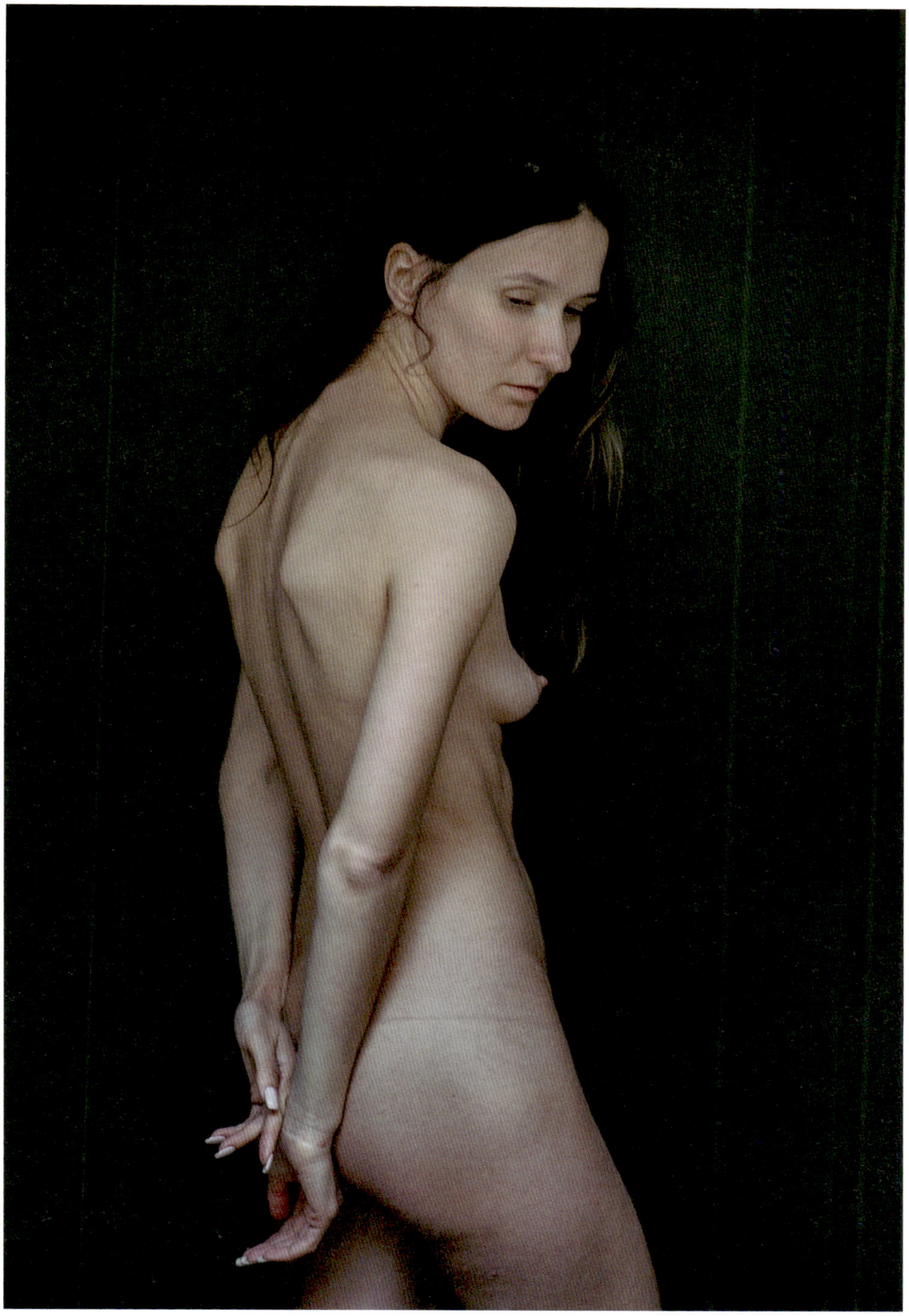

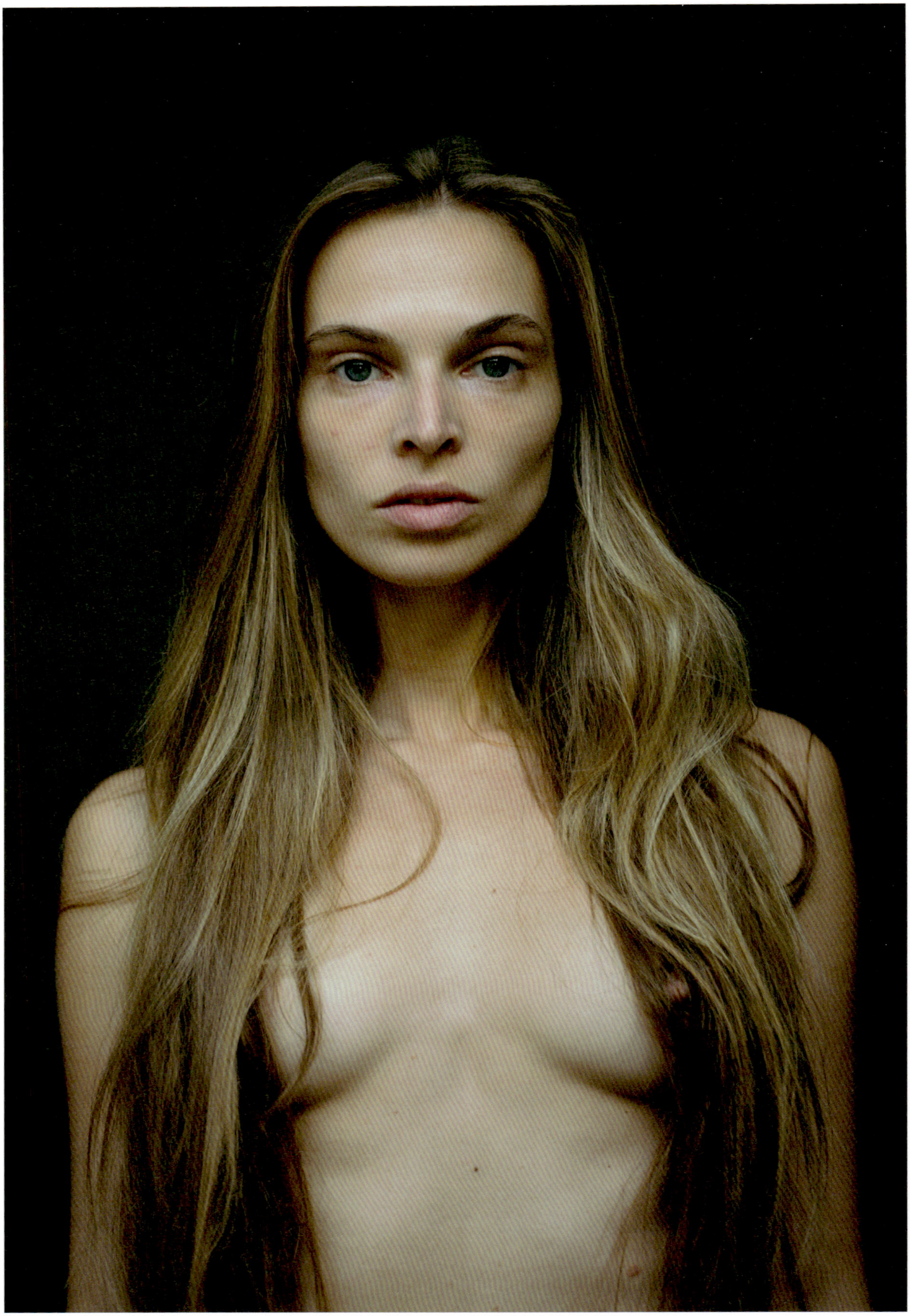

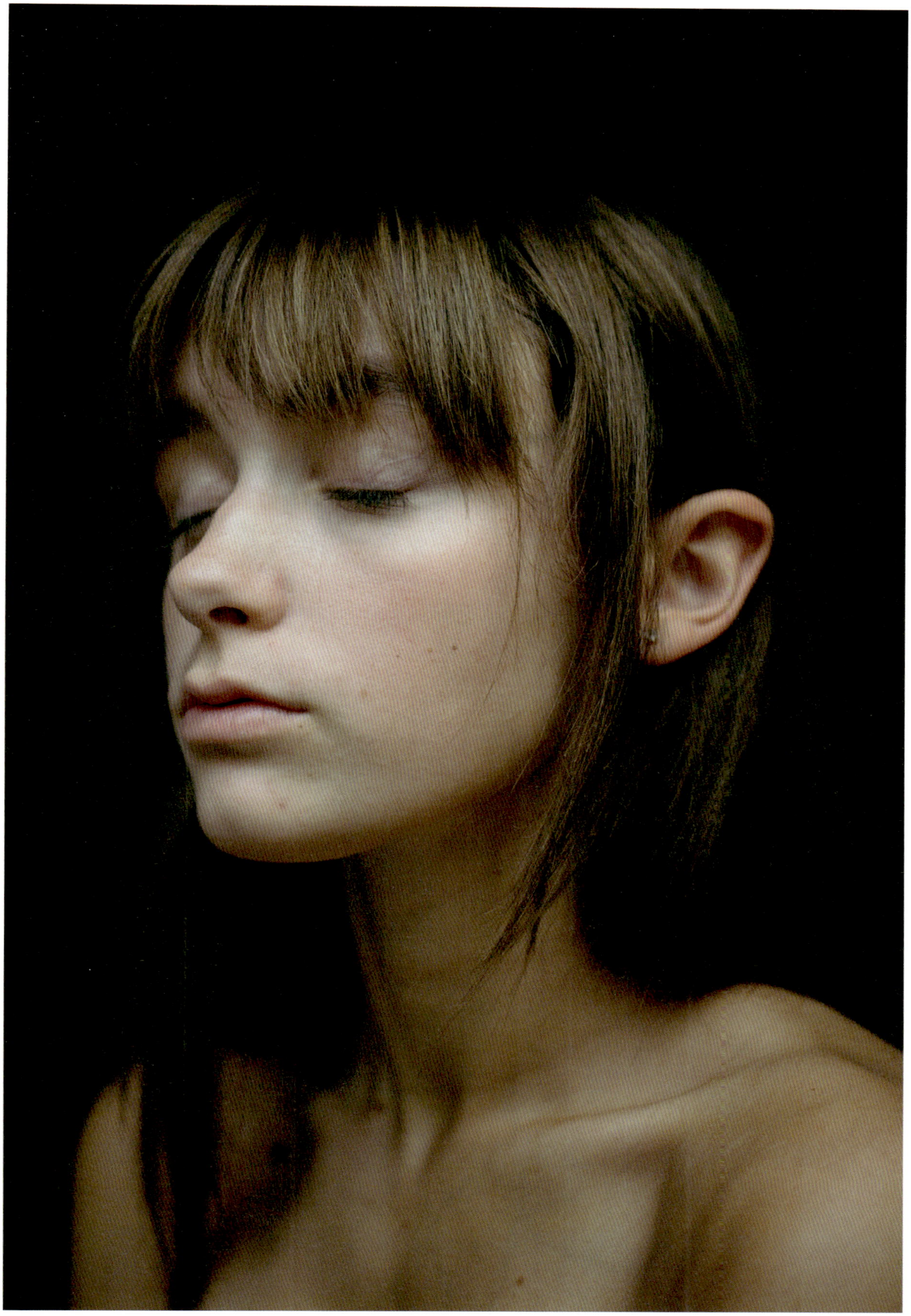

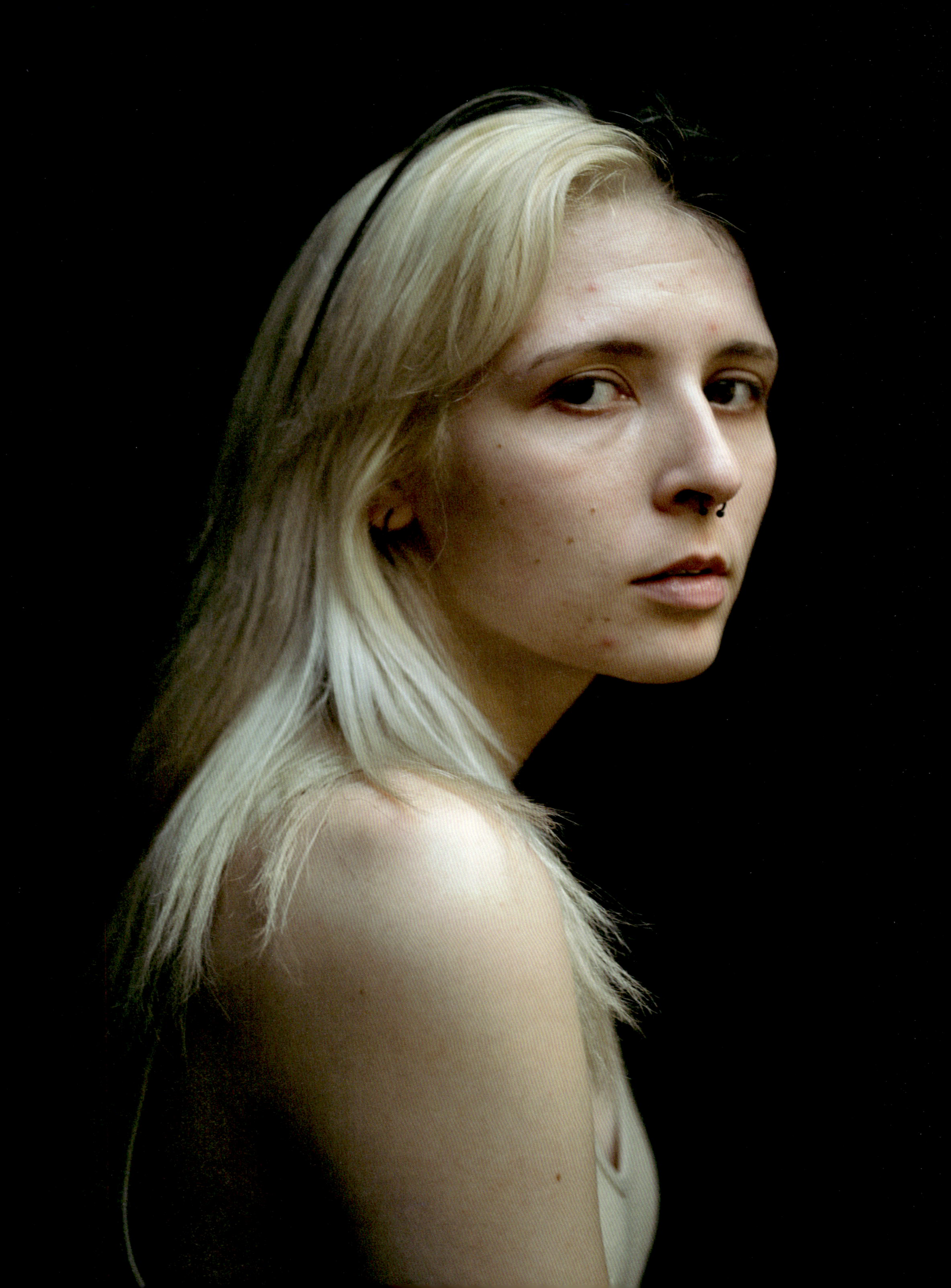

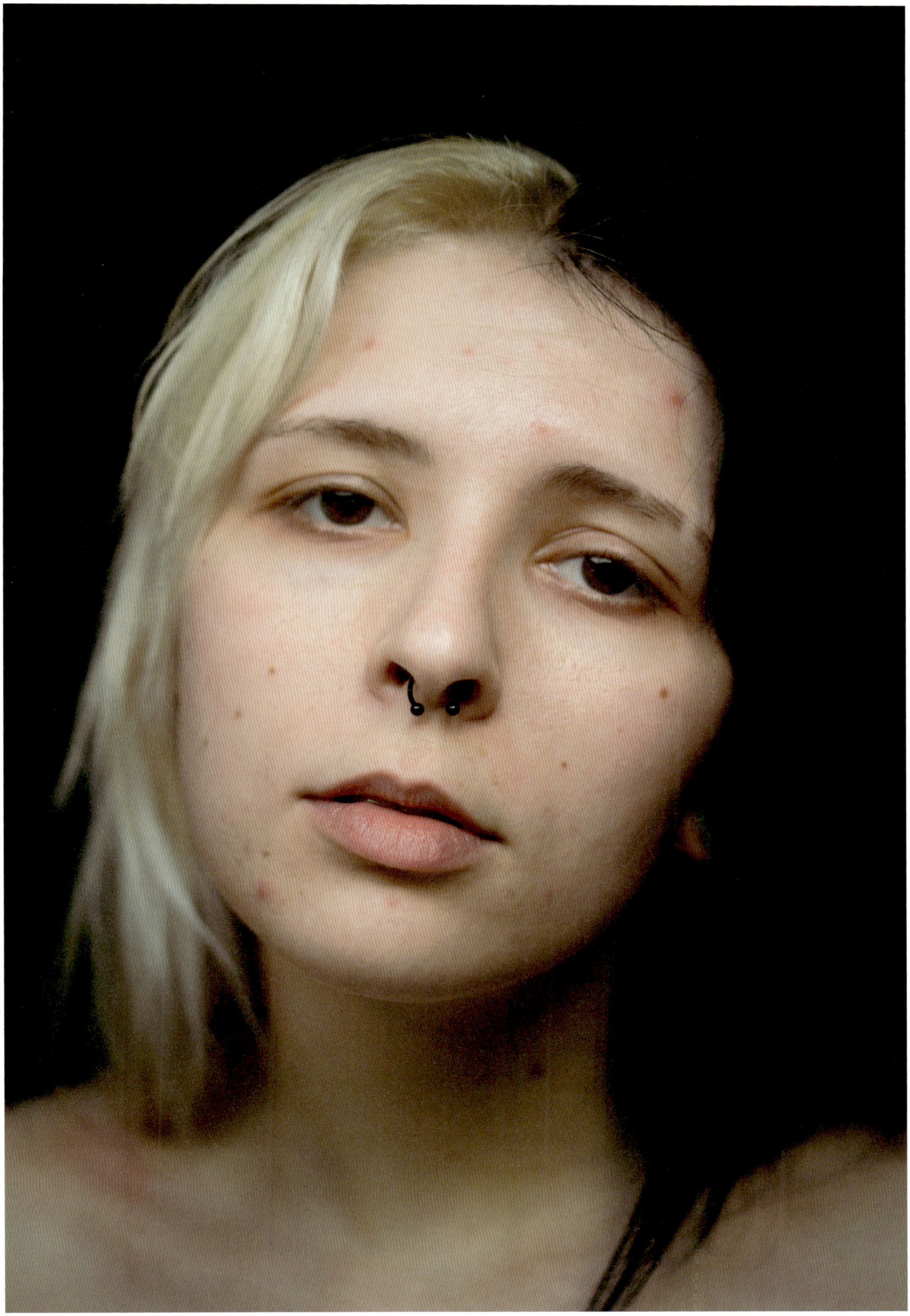

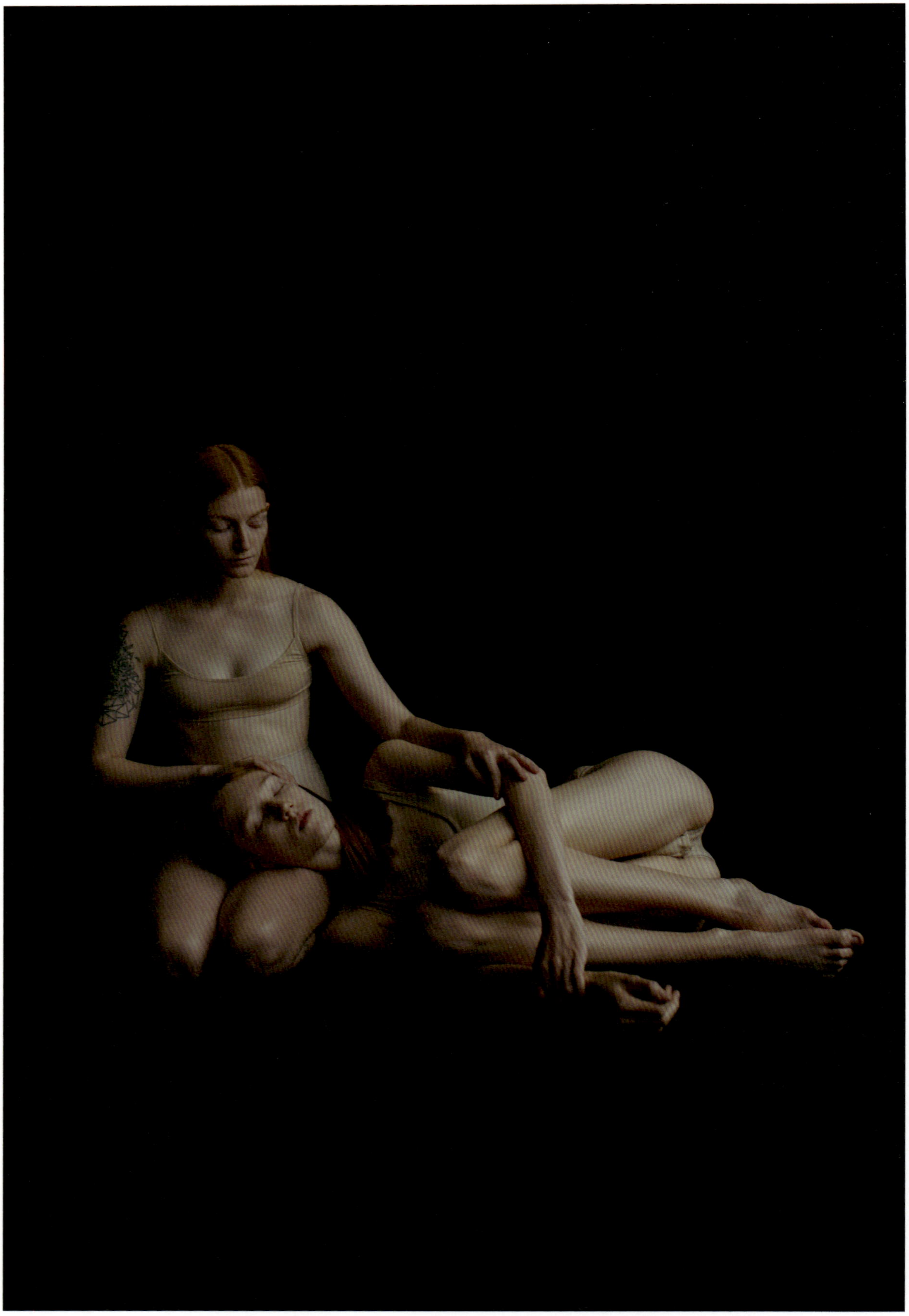

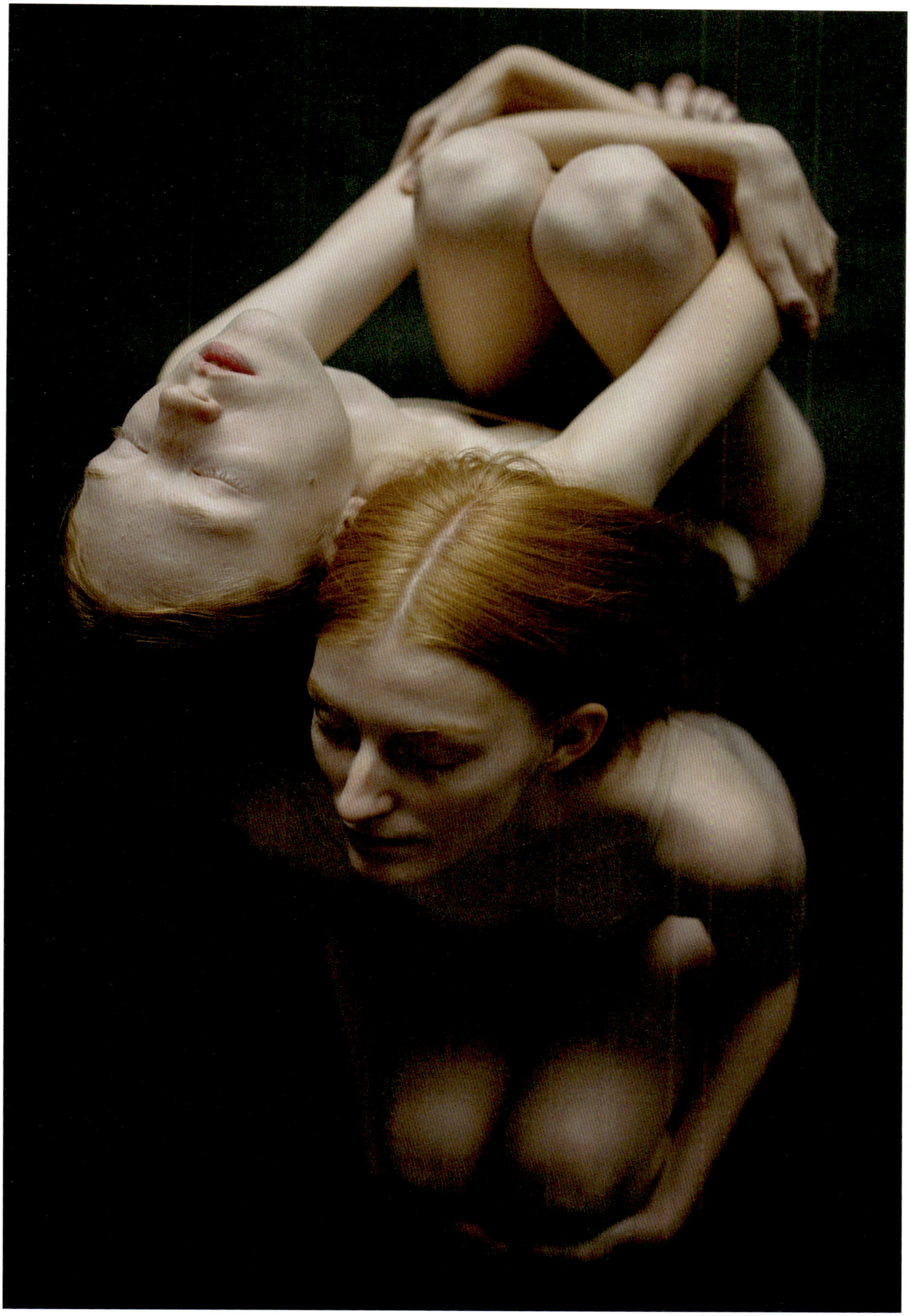

A touch,
A trebled voice,
Goose bumped skin,
Shrinks.
A palette of never seen colours
Unfolds before me,
Unseen
In a mundane sphere.
With closed eyes I stare,
Into the void where the I was once
Engraved.

An emotionless self,
A chaotic breath,
A whispered breeze
Drifting by the Egoic ethos.
A numbed body,
Unanimated.
An inner body,
Joyful.
A tormented mind,
Fades away.
Restless thoughts dissipate,
Arms raise,
Ready to surrender.

The illusion that once fed the fear
Sails away,
Rest remains
Slowly in every tide.
The outer becomes inner.
The assurance that what the I searched
was never lost.
No piece was ever missing.
With an open heart
The I is.

To a safe dock
Waters navigate.
The moon shines
Reflecting true Light.
Soul feels,
Trust guides,
Love never left.
Patiently the being surrenders.
With open heart the I is guided.

In order of appearance:

Elise Gérard
Tazmin Jans
Myrthe Steenbreker
Shari Van der Elst
Melissa Castiau
Laura Ermans
Larissa Matheus
Camille Meuleman
Treaya Davis
Lana Van Deynze
Léa de Wouters
Colette Van Loy
Merel Evers
Barry Ramatou
Andrew Douglas
Guinevere de Rousseau
Marloes van der Donk
Mara Michiels
Carolina Morais
Sandrine Coppens
Yuna Jans
Dovile Paris
Kate Ri

Jasmijn Siau
Xueli Abbing
Elis Stone
Dévale Simao
Zoë Vanbever
Saskia Oever
Joyce Allanois
Nomy van Neerijnen
Mathilde Warnier
Harmonie Tilkens
Stephanie Ballet
Claire Francis
Charisse Van Canneyt
Yasmin Geuens
Ramona Geuens
Ezekiel Chibo
Margot Moerman
Beau Caminada
Annemieke van het Hof
Aster Paleskin
Natasha Schastlivaya
Gaëlle Baekelandt
Kira Kriellaars

emotions *in between* emotions

Published by: Stockmans Art Books
(www.stockmansartbooks.be)
Book design: Tina De Souter
(www.tinadesouter.be)
Photography: Steve Dean Mendes
(www.stevedeanmendes.com)
Poetry: Steve Dean Mendes
Edited by: Bruno Devos
Printed by: Stockmans at Antilope De Bie Printing
Printed on: Arctic Volume White 170 gsm

First edition, printed in an edition of 700 copies

ISBN: 9789464363050

stock
mans
art books